SYNAPTIC ALCHEMY

THE ART AND SCIENCE
of
TURNING IDEAS INTO GOLD

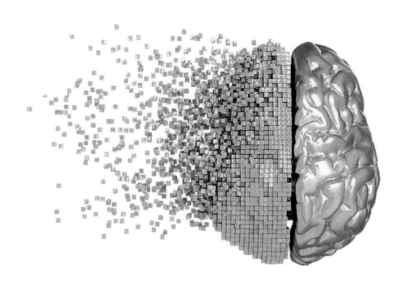

STEVEN CARDINALE

PRAISE FOR SYNAPTIC ALCHEMY

"I love books and ideas that are simultaneously timeless and topical. Synaptic Alchemy effectively applies the classic rites of passage and hero's journey to business and life. Understanding that everything can be distilled down to three stages - ending, creating, scaling - is like receiving a roadmap for wisdom. Highly recommend this book!"

—Chip Conley, Founder of Joie de Vivre Hotels
Founder MEA
Strategic Advisor to Airbnb

"I'm blown away by the hard-won lessons compiled into a clear roadmap. The precious knowledge in this book can save you years of toil. It's easier to get there when you have a roadmap made by an entrepreneur who has already been there at every level."

—Dave Asprey, Founder of Bulletproof
NY Times Author

"Synaptic Alchemy goes to the most fundamental heart of what each of us wants: the skills to turn our ideas into reality. It teaches us the tools and gives us a roadmap to success. I recommend it emphatically. It's a great read!"

—Rick Foster, Global Business Consultant
Co-Author of "How We Choose to Be Happy"

Copies of this book are available at a discount when purchased in quantity for sales promotions, educational or corporate use. Special editions, which include personalized sections, excerpts, and corporate branding are available for large quantities. For more information please contact:

customizedbook@synapticalchemy.com

Get more information about Synaptic Alchemy, courses, blog, podcast at www.SynapticAlchemy.com.

Cataloging-in-Publication Data is available from the Library of Congress.

Printed in the United States of America

ISBN 978-1-7345010-3-2

CONTENTS

FORWARD

It is June 2018 and I am welcoming my 13th cohort of beta guests to MEA, the Modern Elder Academy, which is the world's first "midlife wisdom school." After spending 24 years running Joie de Vivre Hotels, and seven years advising Airbnb on hospitality and strategy, I am very comfortable welcoming guests. I guess that is one of my "superpowers," understanding how to bring people together around a common theme and make them feel centered and at ease.

Steven was in this last cohort and, as all the guests started becoming acquainted, it became apparent that Steven was not here at MEA to simply absorb the teachings. Rather he brought his mind and insights with him to absorb as well as give back by asking better questions. I remember one night he presented his favorite phrase to the group: "A better question is more important than the right answer. Because usually it is the right answer to the wrong question."

What is so powerful about that quote is that usually we are all running to come up with the right answer. The right answer in business. The right answer in our personal lives. The right answer in midlife. The right answer to everything. But, as I am sure you have already intuited, there is no right answer, especially when it comes to transitions such as running a successful business, starting a new venture, or shifting into a new stage of your life.

When it comes to transitioning to the next level of your success you have to go through a "gooey" process (think of the cocoon in the caterpillar to butterfly metamorphosis). You have to cross a liminal threshold. And crossing that threshold does not give you answers, it forces you to have better questions.

That is what Synaptic Alchemy is all about. It is not your typical business book with typical platitudes. Synaptic Alchemy gives you a three-part alchemical transformational process that forces you to ask better questions. That is what is so intriguing about this idea, three simple easy steps that force you to ask better questions that drive your growth towards your next level of success.

It will sound simple: Destroy something, Create something, Scale something. And it is simple. But as you dig deeper into these steps of the alchemical transformation you will notice that you'll be asking yourself the right questions to grow your business or start a new one.

Everyone talks about entrepreneurship and innovation, but there are few new and innovative models out there that give you a new lens to see the world and your decisions. Synaptic Alchemy provides a new framework by reimagining the old masters of transformation, the alchemists. I think that is why this book and this topic are so essential: It shows you a path to success built on the successful questions informed by a millennia old idea, turning ideas into gold.

Chip Conley
Founder and Former CEO
Joie de Vivre Hospitality
Former Head of Global Hospitality & Strategy, Airbnb

DEDICATION

There are certain people who, when they come into your world, change your life and tilt the axis of your universe. People who make you think differently. People who become more than a partner, more than someone you bounce ideas off, more than a collaborator. People who change the way you see the world. People who support your work, are there in the scary times to be by your side, are there with brilliant pushes when the road feels like it is paved with molasses, and share in the celebrations both big and small. Kari Henley is that person. She is my partner, my Beloved, and my light. I'd like to dedicate this book to her in as many ways as an author can dedicate a book.

Expressing my gratitude, joy, and astonishment at having her in my life is something that language lacks, although that is all I have to work with in these pages.

The universe has certainly tilted being by her side; crafting this manuscript, and building a life full of ideas and wonder.

My desire is that everyone who reads this manuscript has a chance to experience the joy and wonder that a true partner like Kari brings.

ACKNOWLEDGMENTS

As professor Scott Galloway from NYU[1] exclaims, "Greatness is achieved in the agency of others. Full stop." There is no truer truth, especially when it comes to the words on these pages.

I think it is vital to acknowledge those who have lifted us on their shoulders, whether or not they know it, and whether or not they know exactly how they accomplished the feat.

There are so many people who have been with me through the crucible of transformation. My sister, Tina Cardinale, has always been there to bounce ideas off. A sibling is a unique relationship because it's one of the only relationships that you carry with you for the vast majority of your life. Without my sister by my side, through the easy and the tough, I would have not gotten to this point in my life, nor been able to ignite the flame that drove this book. Thank you T for all that you are, all that you've given me, and all that you will be.

To my children Alexandra and Nicolai. You have been core to my curiosity, my affection, and my drive to do better in this world. To watch you grow, intellectually spar, and to learn more from you than you could ever know has been one of the true honors of my life. Always being by your side through thick and thin has fine-tuned my spirit to get through the day-to-day process of coming up with this book.

To my cousin Joe. We've known each other since we were little kids. The intellectual gymnastics we participated in as we grew through young adulthood and into our middle years provided me with a springboard from which I was able to jump in creating this work. In fact, Joe came up with the name "Synaptic Alchemy" and consequently deserves all credit where credit is due for giving a name to the concept which is explored at length in these pages.

Then there are the mentors that I find in the ink on the paper of the books in my library or the dots on the screen of my kindle. From academics such as Clayton Christensen, Scott Galloway and Adam Grant to the innovators such as Malcolm Gladwell, Seth Godin and Daniel Pink to the thought leaders such as Geoffrey Moore, Tony Robbins, Dean Graziosi, Tim Ferris and Chip Conley, to my Wharton brethren, and fellow authors such as Dave Asprey and Rick Foster. I have learned so much from so many, and at times, there are just too many mentors to shine light on in these pages. If I missed you here, please know that your ideas and passion are firmly embedded in spirit.

Each and every one of these people has shaped my worldview, my vision, and given me new eyes to see the world and ponder the endless questions. I am more than grateful to all of you, whether I know you personally or only through your pages. My journey through life and through Synaptic Alchemy is because of you. My humblest thanks.

1. What's This All About?

INTRODUCTION

It's late on a Friday afternoon and I have been told by customers, vendors, and employees that the idea I am working on just does not have any legs. It is too complicated for our customers to understand and no one will use it. The team and I are working fifteen hours a day, six days a week.

Maybe I'm delusional and I'm really not making anything customers want. Maybe I'm just creating a project because I think it is cool, but the market is not receptive. Maybe it is just an idea, a dream, a recurring fantastic addiction that keeps pulling me back into the office, back to the drawing board, out of my bed at night to build, build, build. Maybe the naysayers are right. They all say it just isn't going to work ... except for a few.

Except for a few key customers, and a few important individuals that are excited about it. They are excited to see where this all leads. They are excited to see a new product that directly addresses a need they didn't know they had. This is the charge and the electricity that brought me back to my desk every single day.

I knew I was creating something out of thin air that would work. I truly felt like a wild alchemist attempting the impossible in taking mundane, every day systems and turning them into something valuable, new and rare.

It worked. The belief in the impossible paid off and eventually turned into a multi-million-dollar company that impacted my clients, my employees, and all of the lives we touched.

This is the electrical charge of Synaptic Alchemy. The magic of bringing things into being from the recesses of the synapses inside your head. It's what all entrepreneurs are aiming for, whether they know it or not. Entrepreneurs are creators, inventors, builders. They are not just the organizers and directors of businesses. And entrepreneurs that change the way we think have moved into the realm of *Synaptic Alchemists,* pulling ideas down from the heavens to manifest them right here on terra firma.

My job is to help you evolve into the best next iteration of yourself by being part guide, part teacher, and illuminating a trusted success path. My job is to teach you how to think not just differently, but intentionally. To show you how ideas can be turned into gold. To explain the fundamentals of a craft that, while it may appear mysterious on the outside, is readily understandable on the inside. Once you master this craft, you will carry it with you for the rest of your life.

Becoming a Synaptic Alchemist is the key to opening up the next, best version of each of us. If you are like me, you are always looking for that unique gem of insight that guides you to a new level of yourself. If you are like me, I'm sure you have thought: "I know there is something more to my thinking than where I'm at, but what is it?" If you are like me, you are thrilled to have a chance to take time-tested methods from the old masters and see how they are applied by the thought leaders of today.

That is what Synaptic Alchemy is all about. It is a process of thinking, a mindset combined with a path, that can provide you with the competitive advantage you've been looking for. We'll go into the process in great detail to help you understand how the precepts our ancestral alchemists discovered can be paired with today's idea generation techniques. I will teach you how to come up with new and innovative ways of looking at problems, growing a business—whether that business is a startup or a division of a Fortune 500 corporation—and becoming the best version of you as an entrepreneur, executive, or leader.

The Oxford-English dictionary defines an entrepreneur as:

A person who sets up a business or businesses, taking on financial risks in the hope of profit.

While the Merriam-Webster dictionary has a slightly different definition:

One who organizes, manages, and assumes the risks of a business or enterprise.

I disagree.

Both of these definitions are too static, limited and closed. The simplified definition does not reflect the creative nature of what I consider a true entrepreneur.

The business world often defines the character traits of an entrepreneur as that of a Wild West cowboy stereotype. We have heard entrepreneurs:

Possess grit

Require perseverance

Blaze new trails

Take risks

Fred Smith, the founder of FedEx, took the last remaining $5,000 of the company's cash and turned it into $32,000. That took *grit*.

Google founders Larry Page and Sergey Brin tried to sell their technology to Yahoo for $1 million and were turned down. Their desire was to complete their studies at Stanford. Instead they continued along the entrepreneurial path and created Google, whose market cap as of mid 2020 is a little more than $1 trillion (yep, that's a T for Trillion). That required *perseverance*.

Elon Musk took the lion's share of his windfall from the sale of his first company Zip2[2], and eventually helped catapult PayPal into one of the fastest growing internet financial firms. That required him to *blaze a new trail*.

In 2008, while on vacation, Lin-Manuel Miranda[3] read a biography of Alexander Hamilton and then wrote a rap about the founding father. That rap was performed in 2009 at the White House Evening of Poetry, Music, and the Spoken Word with President Barack Obama in the audience. From there, the musical Hamilton evolved from a mixtape to a full-fledged Broadway juggernaut with its first Broadway performance and has now surpassed the $1 billion revenue mark[4].

Creating a Broadway show filled with rap and featuring a cast that was designed to ignore the historical accounts of ethnicity required thinking intentionally and then acting decisively, which is exactly what Miranda did when he *took risks*.

Possessing characteristics of the Wild West or being successful do not, in and of themselves, make you a Synaptic Alchemist. To move into the rarefied air of Synaptic Alchemy you'll need more. The individuals mentioned above not only possess the characteristics of success, they have also crossed into an alchemical way of thinking, whether conscious of it or not.

A Synaptic Alchemist not only needs to Think Differently—as the Apple Computer slogan[5] implies—but must also internalize the two core principles of Synaptic Alchemy:

Think Intentionally & Act Decisively

A Synaptic Alchemist's frame of mind is to conjure the resources and marshal the forces necessary to create a transformation; to understand how to actually imprint ideas on the ground and turn them into golden treasures.

The materials Synaptic Alchemists work with are not ordinary in any fashion. These materials actually don't exist when the process is beginning. The materials they start with

11

come from the synapses in their mind, from the neurons firing inside their head. A Synaptic Alchemist turns an ephemeral idea into gold using not much more than sheer will and passion. And in today's society, it is the Synaptic Alchemist who wins everything.

The modern business world is all about mining gold from ideas. This is especially true in the technology sector, where Google, Facebook, eBay, Instagram, Amazon, Intel, Microsoft, and Apple are all examples of Synaptic giants of the tech world. But this is not the only way Synaptic Alchemy can work.

Synaptic Alchemy is handcrafted every day by individuals just like you in art, science, business and activism. Sometimes it is done with intention and sometimes by accident. But make no mistake, any individual can learn the Intentional Thinking and Acting Decisively concepts necessary to become a Synaptic Alchemist. You will learn in this book how to apply the strategies, interpret the language, and develop the right mindset to become one yourself.

Alchemy is about capturing lightning in a bottle, but not just by building something tangible. Alchemy is about nurturing and shepherding a transformation. That transformation might be turning lead into gold by turning an ephemeral idea into a living, breathing reality, or transforming your mind or body from where you are now to where you want to be.

Synaptic Alchemy, as described in this book, is not just a mindset. It is a way of thinking. I'm not referring just to feel good motivation. It takes more than simply thinking positive thoughts or consuming motivational videos on YouTube to become a Synaptic Alchemist. It takes doing. It takes creating. Experimenting with spaces in between *what-is* and *what-will-be*. A new reality is forged as you close the gap between *what-is* and *what-will-be*. It takes paying attention to where you are and where you want to be and living in the crucible of fire that is liminal transformation.

Here's the great thing. People have been playing with the fire of alchemy for centuries. We tend to think of alchemy as this grandiose pursuit of early scientists and inventors— innovators of the ancient and pre-modern worlds. As impressive as their ambitions were, no one REALLY can melt down some ordinary lead and turn it into liquid gold. The actual task of turning lead into gold, historically a primary objective of alchemists in the West, is not what we are after.

Alchemy, for the purposes of this book, is the PROCESS of bringing new things to life. And the alchemists of the past have created a blueprint for you to work through, so you don't have to just wing it.

Their efforts spanned hundreds, possibly even thousands, of years, giving these mythic legends the time to create a process for transformation that could stand the test of time.

Because alchemy has a mystical, rather than practical, reputation today, this process, this set of creative principles, is largely unknown.

This book intends to change that by reintroducing and revitalizing these ancient concepts, and presenting an updated version of the alchemical process designed for the modern era: Synaptic Alchemy.

Becoming a Synaptic Alchemist is what it takes to leapfrog to the front of the success queue in today's world. My vision for you is that, by acquiring the mindset and tools of the Synaptic Alchemist, you will turbo charge your dreams and success.

ANCIENT WISDOM +
MODERN OPPORTUNITY

The concept of Synaptic Alchemy didn't just strike like lightning. I didn't just wake up one day and suddenly exclaim: "alchemy is exactly like the principles of innovation and entrepreneurship." Nope, nothing like that.

What did happen, however, is even more powerful. It is what happens when the truth slowly seeps into your consciousness over time. I have been studying innovation, entrepreneurship and startups for years. Reading books like "The Innovator's Dilemma," "The Lean Startup," "Crush it," and "Purple Cow." You name it, I read it. I was fascinated by the process of taking ideas and creating something tangible from them. Even though I didn't realize it back then, that was the start of my journey to uncovering Synaptic Alchemy.

But you can explore a topic only so far just by reading about it. You have to get into the ring and really meet that topic face-to-face to truly understand it. That's what I've been doing since I was very young. Coming up with ideas and trying to imprint them on the ground as businesses. The successes, and the failures, that resulted from these ideas paved the way for me to learn what innovation and entrepreneurship really mean in today's world.

As I'm sure you are aware, this time in history is moving at such an accelerated pace that if you don't have a good path you'll likely spend a significant chunk of time banging into brick walls and going nowhere. Luckily, from the perspective of learning from one's mistakes, that's exactly what I did. I banged into so many brick walls that I probably have an imprint of bricks on my forehead.

That's the on-the-ground educational process as it applies today. Build fast, fail faster, consume as much learning as you can from others who have already done it or studied it, whether that learning comes from books, audio, conferences, newsletters, in person—you name it. Combine that with learning on the ground about technology, finance, operations, HR, marketing and executing at businesses and you have the experimental cocktail that gave me an edge. It framed the window on the opportunities we all have in today's fast-paced world.

The alchemy part didn't surface until my cousin spoke the term: Synaptic Alchemy. That's what I was doing whether I knew it or not. I was, and still am, an alchemist of ideas, trying to cast gold from the most powerful resource I have: my mind.

Once the name Synaptic Alchemy was in the air it stuck, and I started to wonder exactly what the alchemists of yore really worked on? Was it just the magic of turning lead into gold? Over the next five years, little-by-little, I started to explore alchemy. I found all sorts of strange and esoteric stuff to read and explore. I found all sorts of attempts to actually turn lead into gold. I also found stuff on trying to achieve immortality via an elixir of eternal youth. Then I stumbled upon Carl Jung's Red Book.

Image 1 - Carl Jung - The Red Book

Carl Jung, the Swiss psychiatrist and father of analytical psychology, had a pressing question expressed through a series of reflections in the early 1900's. His question, "what is the myth of my life?" led him to discover that both the myth of his life and the myth of the Red Book were the same myth—the alchemical myth. The Red Book itself is the story of Jung's confrontation with the unconscious and his exploration of psychological individuation (the process of growing and maturing into a well-functioning whole[6]).

As I read and started to understand Jung's dive into alchemy—an approach that had nothing to do with turning one metal into another but rather centered on a human transformation—Synaptic Alchemy started to take shape. It was at that point that I really understood that alchemy was not a formula, but rather a path of transformation. An inner shift.

It's the same transformation I had been learning about from all those books and authors when it came to innovation and business. But instead of just lofty ideas, alchemy had a path, a process. It had steps that led to a mindset.

So, take the path, the steps of an alchemical transformation that the old masters used to try to find the gold in lead, combine those steps with modern theories of innovation and entrepreneurship, and voila: Synaptic Alchemy.

Why This Book

There are thousands of books on business, entrepreneurship, innovation, marketing, the digital economy, and strategy. Some of these books provide a deep dive on a specific topic. Others have an academic point of view. A few reflect the experiences of a single entrepreneur being in the trenches and figuring out what worked and what didn't, and then focusing on a specific strategy or set of tactics applicable to advertising, sales, or marketing.

When writing this book, I realized we don't need more tactics. There is a plethora of books on the next trend in social media or how to close sales. We don't need more academic literature on macro business models on strategy for an entire sector or how to analyze a public company's financials. And we definitely don't need more books on what made one entrepreneur's idea successful. We need something ancient. Something archetypal. Something mystical to combine with the practical. Something alchemical.

This book is designed to give you a mental model, framework, and mindset you'll need to become successful at whatever venture you undertake. Intentional Thinking will become your mantra. Decisive Action will be your guide. From there you will be armed with the knowledge of concepts that can make all the difference in launching the next blockbuster product in your industry. Starting a life-changing business or promoting a social idea all require strategy. This book can help you gain the long-range vision that you need to keep moving through the various ups and downs of the daily tactics.

Synaptic Alchemy is both an internal mindset and an operational strategy that you can use to guide you on a daily basis. If properly utilized, it is a powerful approach to getting where you want to go.

As a Synaptic Alchemist you can:

- Discover the next idea to take your company from good to great

- Build a breakthrough product to take your company from functioning to extraordinary

- Create a life-changing business, project, system or creative endeavor

- Unite teams or groups around a common cause

- Grow your idea and your impact 10x, 100x, or 1,000x by understanding core concepts

The academic business models are great at giving you a macro big picture understanding of what is going on. I should know, I am constantly reading, listening, watching, and consuming as much academic literature as I can get my hands on, not only when I was at business school, but now many years later as a professional. But the academic models are so big they don't necessarily give you the map you need.

The flood of tactical advice outlines details of the current landscape. The day-to-day operational models of digital advertising, paid search or social media all provide clarity on how things work at the micro level. But the micro level is not strategic. The micro level lets you know what next step to take for something specific, but it doesn't give you a model for success.

That's "Why This Book." This book is designed to give you a big-picture macro model that you can refer to every single day as a vision that also drives your micro actions.

That's what we need. Synaptic Alchemy offers: macro vision - connected to - micro execution.

This gives you a powerful mental framework for achieving your goals.

A macro long-term vision (Intentional Thinking) gives you a North Star guided direction to set your course and micro execution (Decisive Action) helps you figure out what next step to take to spin the *lead* of ideas into the *gold* of success.

THE ALCHEMICAL STORY

Naturally, before we can begin with the tactical recipe of how to become a Synaptic Alchemist, we have to start with a story.

We all know a good story when we hear one. The kind of story that makes you sit up straight, stop whatever you are doing and pay attention. The kind of story that stops you in your tracks and makes you realize that everything else you've been paying attention to is just noise, that this is a story worth listening to. If you are a *Game of Thrones* fan you may recall this moment in one of the most popular pop culture events of the 2010's, the finale of *Game of Thrones*[7] when Tyrion Lannister gave the following speech:

"What unites people? Armies? gold? Flags? No. It's stories. There's nothing in the world more powerful than a good story. Nothing can stop it. No enemy can defeat it."

—Tyrion Lannister – *Game of Thrones* finale

Although he is talking about who should rule in a fictional realm after a fictional war, his idea is nonetheless a point well taken.

In today's day and age, where we swipe and scroll through the feed of our collective lives with astonishing speed, what better to slow us down, or stop us in our tracks, then a captivating story. Story has been a driving factor since theatrical players first took the stage in ancient Greece in the Theater of Dionysus, built in the shadow of the Acropolis in Athens at the beginning of the 5th century BCE[8].

Image 2 - Theatre of Dionysos Eleuthereus, Athens, by Mark Cartwright

It is story that drives people to action and story that enables people to remember and engage.

In the book *Made to Stick: Why Some Ideas Survive and Others Die*[9] Dan & Chip Heath present some compelling evidence as to where and why story matters. Chip Heath teaches a class at Stanford University. One of the lessons he gives his students is to create presentations on crime patterns. He provides them with the statistics. Half the class must give a presentation supporting the claim that non-violent crime IS a serious problem and the other half must present the argument that non-violent crime is NOT a serious problem. Your traditional pro / con presentation on a concept. Then comes the twist: the twist about stories. The students are then shown a short 10-minute video designed to distract them, after which they are asked to recall the presentations they just heard 10 minutes ago.

> "When students were asked to recall the speeches,
> 63 percent remember the stories.
> Only 5 percent remember any individual statistic."
> —Chip Heath

63 percent vs. 5 percent of students remember story over stats. That's a pretty impressive chasm. But why? Why do we remember stories more than just concepts or facts? And why do certain stories surface in our minds more frequently than others?

A story answers a fundamental question in the audience's mind, heart and spirit. It answers with power and conflict. It answers with emotional charge. We are wired for story in a fundamental way. Good stories engage not only our intellect but our emotions as well and that is why we remember them. As well as being powerful, they *feel* powerful.

Alchemical stories are about the change from one state to another. From the perspective of storytelling, alchemical stories are about the conversion of a character who seems just like us into a character that feels like the next, best version of us. Alchemical stories are about changing a characteristic of humanity that feels like lead into the gold of a better version of ourselves. Alchemical stories are all about self-discovery.

If you are a fan of Fantasy genre movies, then you are likely familiar with the story of the Hobbit, who is another hidden Synaptic Alchemist. The story of the Hobbit recounts the quest of Bilbo Baggins from a life of quiet rural peace through many adventures to his ultimate encounter with Smaug the dragon. He emerges from these adventures entirely different from when he started, with strengths, gifts and qualities he never imagined he possessed.

Bilbo starts off on the journey content with his life. Content with the peace of the Shire. Who of us hasn't longed for that type of contentment? That gentle peace that we imagine could envelop us as long as the outside world is kept at bay.

However, we all know the reality of the world. It will not let us rest for too long. The outside world either beckons us to adventure, or directly intrudes on our solitude, just like it did with Bilbo. Metaphorically speaking, we've all known our own dragons, whether they are internal or external. We also all have known at some pivotal point in our life, deep in our gut, that we are going to have to grow and mature into the next iteration of ourselves. We know we will have to face and conquer these dragons—they will not vanish on their own.

That's an alchemical story. A story of transformation. That is what all alchemists conjure—stories of transformation. These are the stories that are spun into our favorite movies and into our ears as an audience in such a way that two things come to mind:

1.) That's just like me. The character has something that I viscerally relate to and can understand. Or, the story has something that I can viscerally relate to and understand.

2.) There is a transformation that connects to me. A transformation that I recognize or have a hunger for.

We fell in love with Bilbo Baggins, the Hobbit because he was someone we could all relate to. That is one of the secrets of a Synaptic Alchemist. Their inner transformation is so clear for everyone to see, they end up taking us right along with them.

Let's explore a modern-day alchemist that you might already know.

Oprah Winfrey is clearly a Synaptic Alchemist. She started her life as an everyday woman, and despite her success in television, movies and magazines, she excels at being real. She connects alchemically with her audience, because she doesn't sit above them. She sits with them. Oprah and her audience become one in sharing a common story. Yes, we all know that she has buckets of money and millions of fans. But we can also feel that her struggles, her hopes, her dreams are just like us. As she becomes one with her audience, so does her alchemical story.

Oprah feels an intimate connection with her fans. This connection is a key to the transformation she shepherds. Why? Because the alchemical *lead* that transforms into *gold* is the same color and texture for her as the *lead* her audience has at home. She transforms whatever she is interested in (which is the same stuff her audience is interested in), into *gold,* whether it was her "favorite things", book clubs or Super Soul Sunday podcast.

Each and every effort she undertakes evolves into an alchemical conversion from the *lead* of her ideas into the *gold* of impact. When she interviews Eckhart Tolle, the author of *The Power of Now*, we feel her spirit opening up, and she shows that transformation to her audience, and then takes us with her as an everyday person working hard to learn, grow and understand. That's an alchemical story.

Learning how to do this isn't easy. Typically, our own life story does not begin as an alchemical one. More often than not, we start off with a rather ordinary story that looks a lot like every day *lead*. Then, we are fashioned by the circumstances and situations of life that begin to heat us up and inspire the alchemical process to begin.

I remember when I first went to college. I was living someone else's story, and there was nothing alchemical about it. I was living the story of my parents, of middle-class American society, and my own naive drives. I was at UCLA studying Biochemistry, and I hated it. I put in hours and hours trying to memorize and understand the concepts. I was fully consumed with the story of going to medical school as my path; and this was the track that got you there. I soon realized I was living someone else's story.

When people would ask me the typical bland conversation starter of, "what are you up to?" I couldn't answer. My answers were pulled from a bag of responses that included "taking classes" or "studying for finals," but I couldn't conjure up a story that mattered. After a couple of years, I quit taking pre-med courses. It wasn't me. I never had the fire and passion to complete the required trajectory to achieve success in the medical field.

Unsure of my direction, or what would be my alchemical *lead* in life, one day I stumbled into an economics class. It changed my life. My first true alchemical wizard was waiting there for me. He transformed my impression of economics from the lead of boring numbers to the absolute gold of stories. He said, "economics is not the study of money. Economics is the study of choice. The things you consciously choose, and the things you don't think you have a choice in; like who your kids are, what family you belong to, or when you are going to die."

That was it. Those words completely changed my direction.

I switched my major to Economics and started getting in the driver's seat of my future. I came to life. I began playing fast paced, betting-style chess games for money, and I tasted success and competition. I learned the game of thinking intentionally and acting decisively.

I worked my way into computer programming jobs by spending every hour I could reading coding books from scratch. I had zero experience in programming but figured out how to program what I needed in real time. I would read a chapter on coding and implement it while working on the night shift and continue Econ classes during the day.

I learned a simple lesson: either what I learned worked and the computer did what I asked of it, or not. The 'or not' would end up with long debugging sessions and black or blue screens filled with errors. Computers are very quick to let you know if you are doing it right or not.

By my senior year I was running a small computer management business out of my campus apartment with employees crammed into my tiny space, and making $20K per month. The work in learning computers, and the gift of hustle were paying off, and none of that had anything to do with my major. This was economics in real life. The lead was turning into gold.

I became interested in all aspects of business, personal growth and personal development, and all of that lit a fire in my belly that has lasted for 40 years. The story of applying technology, concepts and passion to change and motivate the world was my personal alchemical story. One small shift in how I was thinking about what I wanted to do with my life, combined with a huge hunger to bring that shift into reality, would change my personal *lead* into *gold*.

Let's take a moment here and pause. What's your story? What moment in your life served as an alchemical transformation? It is important to reflect on your past for these fundamental shifts and pivots. All good Synaptic Alchemists weave fundamental stories for themselves and for their ideas. An alchemical story is the ONLY story that will resonate with your customers, your audience and you personally. And that's the story of transformation that is about to be woven for you.

IT'S ALL IN MY HEAD

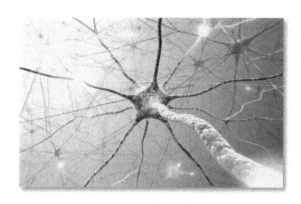

An alchemical story, like the one mentioned in the last section, is a vital component of your journey. But what is your story about? Great and memorable stories are about transformation. Of moving from where you are to where you want to be. But what kind of transformation is it?

Your story could be about a physical transformation. We all love the story of the youngster who overcomes his physical limitations to defeat the bully. That story is a time-tested physical transformation story that never gets old, and one that I experienced myself as a scrawny kid who was picked on and beaten up by the school bully. Until I studied martial arts over a summer, came back to school four inches taller, confident in my self-defense skills, and confronted the bully once and for all.

You might know the movie "The Karate Kid." The story of Daniel, a teenager, who is harassed by a group of bullies.

34

Finding the right sage and teacher, Daniel transforms his skills as a fighter and is eventually able to vanquish the bullies in a martial arts tournament.

That's a physical transformation. Something that we viscerally understand. I have continued to practice martial arts, so it is also a story that I personally relate to. However, there is a more powerful transformation that occurred for Daniel the character and I in real life. A different form of transformation that always must happen either prior to or during the physical transformation.

Changing your body is one thing. But your body is not your only tool, and in the modern world physicality does not transform you. The key transformation lies in:

Changing Your Mind

Proactively adjusting your mindset, how you think, how you perceive the world, is the change that will make all the difference. True change is all in your head.

That's the Synaptic part of Synaptic Alchemy. Scientists have discovered that there are as many neurons in the human brain as there are stars in the Milky Way galaxy. I've heard it said that there are about 100 billion neurons in the brain. Each of those neurons is connected to other brain cells via synapses which are a junction between two nerve cells. The number of connection estimates vary depending on the source, but I've seen averages of $7,000^{10}$ synapses per neuron. The estimates are around 2×10^{14} synapses in your brain.

That means changing your mind could be looked at like changing the path of the stars in the Milky Way. A huge feat. If done right, it yields huge results: sometimes results that are unimaginable.

We've all heard the stories of people who made intentional decisions to get healthy and then dropped 100 pounds. David Goggins, the American runner, author and former Navy Seal, has an astonishing story that he recounts in his book "Can't Hurt Me: Master Your Mind and Defy the Odds."[11] Goggins changed his mind and moved from his painful past of being overweight, depressed and unclear of his future, to becoming an elite athlete as well as losing 106 pounds in three months.

Yes, his transformation was physical. Yes, he had to put in the work, the dedication, the devotion, and intense physical effort. But before all that happened, he had to change his mind. He wanted to be a Navy Seal, and he made up his mind to do what it took to achieve that goal. In changing his mind, he changed his circumstances, enabling him to leave his past behind and lose over 100 pounds in ninety days, and indeed become both a Navy Seal and so much more.

This is what a change in your synapses can do. It is an intentional change to how you link concepts in your mind. It is a change in how your synapses understand relationships. It is an intentional decision process to take your 2×10^{14} synaptic connections and understand and affect the world differently.

This is the Synaptic part of Synaptic Alchemy. Alchemists of the past were looking to change something physical into something else physical: lead into gold. Synaptic Alchemists of today seek to take ideas from their minds and use them to change the way the world works and how they themselves see and understand the world, thereby spinning gold threads from thin air.

BIG PICTURE &&& LITTLE STEPS

Let's talk about how *Intentional Thinking* in the big picture of things or as macro vision ties into all alchemical ideas. Indeed, it is crucial to prioritize this before you even consider taking *Decisive Action*, which often shows up as the little steps, or as micro execution.

Let's face it, a big picture idea is singular, and the steps to get there are many. Prepare yourself for the &&&. Strap on your alchemist apron and get into the foundry. Let's start melting stuff and see what happens.

Putting one foot in front of the other (micro execution) is the only way we make progress towards our goals. But taking step after step doesn't do us much good if we don't know in which direction we should be walking (macro vision).

To paraphrase personal development coach Tony Robbins,

"if you are running East looking for a sunset, I don't care how enthusiastic you are, it's not going to happen—you have the wrong strategy."

That a key strategy to remember in Synaptic Alchemy: Macro Vision guides Micro Execution. Thomas Edison was a Synaptic Alchemist. He had a vision of commercializing[12] the electric lightbulb (macro vision). With this Intentional Thinking, he combined various glass, tubes, and wiring materials together for years, in over a thousand experiments, (micro execution of Acting Decisively) before it finally worked. He bottled light. He spun lead into gold.

Big Picture + Little Steps = true progress towards your North Star.

Do you have a big idea gnawing at you? Are you ready to apply Intentional Thinking to that idea? Are you disciplined enough to Act Decisively on the lessons you will learn in these pages?

You'll have to take many, many little steps if your big picture is truly big. Your little steps will have to be in direct alignment with your big picture. It may be hard. There will be failures, disappointment and setbacks. But consider the alternative of NOT trying.

If Thomas Edison decided to bail at experiment #998 we would still be lighting candles at night.

If you are inspired by a big idea, and embrace your own personal alchemical process, you too will have the chance to turn your ideas into gold.

How to Use This Book

Now that you have some background and basic language tools in your tool belt, we can begin. The Alchemical Process is the core of this book. It will be the key to turning your ideas into gold.

I've broken down alchemy into two core segments:

- Know Yourself

- The Alchemical Transformation

This makes implementing the entire idea of something rather complex like Synaptic Alchemy into something extremely easy once you get the hang of it. I will go through each of the steps of the alchemical process in detail as the book progresses. Getting the core concepts under your fingers and into your DNA will allow you to effectively apply the model to your life on a day-to-day basis.

There are two points of view required to implement our Big Picture &&& Little Steps:

1. **Big Picture Concepts:** At each step of the alchemical process, you'll find an in-depth discussion that describes the big concepts associated with that part of the process. I strongly recommend taking a good chunk of time to get these big picture concepts under your fingertips since understanding the foundational concepts will be key to orienting the direction you will be following when you take little steps.

2. **Little Steps**: The steps you take every day to move towards your goal align with your big picture concepts. Each step in itself moves you a little further along your alchemical path. As you read through these pages you'll find exercises, points of view, or activities that guide you on your step-by-step progress. The little steps are the tangible ways you move on your path and are aligned with the big picture concepts.

You have the power within you for greatness. You have an inspiration, an idea, a process that is whispering to you from the ether. You can become a Synaptic Alchemist.

WHO IS THIS BOOK FOR?

Well, the first and easiest answer is everyone. But sometimes an answer like everyone is as useless as no one. Synaptic Alchemy works across industries, titles, and positions because it is not a set of tactics. It is a unique way to apply a modern strategic mindset, based on ancient principles, to the process of idea manifestation.

Ideas are brought to life in all sorts of areas, from the product innovation groups of big companies, to the human resources of Fortune 500 companies, to entrepreneurs and startups, to public policy teams, etc. Your position, where you work, and what your ultimate goals are don't affect your ability to apply the principles of Synaptic Alchemy to create a different mindset.

Whether you are in a Fortune 100 company, a Startup, part of a Non-Profit, are a Developing Entrepreneur, or part of a

Political campaign, the ideas covered in this book will give you a path to create lasting transformation

You may say to yourself, *"I'm already a senior executive"* or, *"I have an MBA from a prestigious school"* so … *"I don't need this book. I already know how to innovate."* Maybe that is true. Maybe you are great at innovation and coming up with great new ideas. However, most corporations and business schools show and teach how to deliver existing products and services more efficiently and at a lower cost. They are not designed to teach people how to be better at discovery.[13] And discovery is what Synaptic Alchemy is all about.

Synaptic Alchemists are:

Leaders: The ability to motivate or inspire everything from a small group to an organization of thousands requires a unique mindset. It requires intention to change the hearts and minds of those who look to you for leadership. Synaptic Alchemy is, by definition, the transformation of thoughts. Having a formalized structure around the delivery of leadership makes all the difference between intentional success and just hoping to inspire.

Innovators: Whether you have a new invention or idea, are moving a large, successful organization to a different path, or are creating new products and services for your customers as a startup, being able to innovate with a strategy is vital. Embracing the strategic direction innovation requires, without blocking idea generation, is what Synaptic Alchemy is all about. It is big picture strategy combined with next step execution.

Operations Executives and Employees: Sometimes we assume that new concepts, ideas or ways of thinking are only for entrepreneurs in startups or small companies with an entrepreneurial spirit. That couldn't be further from the truth. Just because an organization has procedures and processes, meetings and committees, doesn't mean that a strategic transformational mindset can't apply. Integrating an alchemical mindset in these organizations takes place within the constructs of the organizational structure, and at times will be the ONLY way to move your team forward.

Product Developers: Product managers, developers, engineers, and scientists all need to think through new ways to create products, take ideas from the drawing board and breathe life into blueprints. The traditional way of creating products along with the new processes of product development work well in most circumstances. However, can you imagine how much further you could go if you had access to a powerful overarching strategy? A strategy that may take you in a completely different direction, enabling you to come up with a completely new and innovative product? This is where Synaptic Alchemy fits in.

Startups: The startup world is filled with ideas, innovation and endless energy. Sometimes that energy and those ideas have a clear strategy behind them with a viable direction. However, many times they are explosive creative bursts that don't necessarily have a unique strategic path to success. That is where Synaptic Alchemy can make the difference. The strategic steps that have been handed down through the ages provide a framework for startups—a strategic direction—that can make all the difference.

Entrepreneurs: At times entrepreneurs and startups feel synonymous. However, they don't have to go hand-in-hand. The entrepreneurial spirit is something that is internal. It is a drive to discover and create, not unlike the drive of the explorer: The drive to experience the thrill of exploring caverns or climbing mountains, whether those are physical or in your mind, is part of the entrepreneurial spirit. However, like those involved in startups, without a big picture vision and a strategic direction, without asking the right questions, entrepreneurs can spend a significant amount of time on a path that leads to a dead end—the proverbial road to nowhere. The alchemical process can short-circuit those dead-ends and increase the likelihood that you will find your unique path.

Professionals: Many professionals: doctors, lawyers, accountants, engineers, teachers, firefighters, law enforcement, and others, might think that they don't have access to the alchemical process. That the constraints of their profession preclude them from thinking differently. This is not the case. Just because you have to practice your craft in a specific way does not mean that you cannot include alchemical thinking in your day-to-day work. In fact, it is this alchemical thinking that will inform your work and allow you to stand out from the crowd.

Political Figures: Since the Westernized caricature of alchemy is to turn lead into gold, many will believe that alchemical thinking is only for those in business. Not true. There is nothing more alchemical than changing the hearts and minds of the public or convincing fellow legislators to agree to a higher value. The trick is to think like an alchemist in a political world and not a politician in an alchemical world. The lead of old ideas can quickly be transformed into the gold of new policy given the right strategic framework.

THE ECONOMICS OF ALCHEMY

Earlier, I spoke about my alchemical transformation when I was in the trenches at UCLA studying something I hated. I signed up for my very first Economics class at UCLA as a general elective. I was with a bunch of other students thinking that by studying Economics I would be studying money and by some strange twist of logic I assumed that studying money would lead to a lifetime of wealth. The class was filled with students all driven by this same fallacy, filled with hopes of conquering the financial and material terrain and waiting with bated breath for the professor's monetary magic to enlighten us all.

What we were all expecting was some Gandalf-like wizard, brimming with financial spells, to walk in the door. What we actually experienced was something completely unexpected. What we got was an older, heavyset, professorial curmudgeon who quickly dispelled any ideas that we would all get rich. The first few phrases that came out of our professor's mouth would drastically alter the trajectory of my career as well as my understanding of the basics of my assumptions.

As I mentioned earlier, our curmudgeonly Gandalf stand-in said the following:

> "No one here is going to get rich by studying economics, so stop thinking you are. Economics is not the study of wealth. Economics is the study of choice. Things in which you don't think you have choice. Like when you are going to die, who your children are, and how happy you will be."

That statement hit me like a ton of bricks. "Economics is the study of choice." Who thinks that? What's even more interesting is that it is true. It IS the study of choice. And what's even more fascinating is that we have choice, we have agency, about things that we never thought we could affect.

The ability to affect choice, to affect the path that our lives take, and not just our emotional lives but our economic lives as well, is key to the entrepreneurial drive. But how? How do we affect our paths? What are the key drivers to a new path and how do we know what the markers of a new path look like?

This has always been a struggle for me. The entrepreneur, the cowboy spirit pushing on the frontiers incessantly looks for a new path. Unfortunately, most of the time we spin fruitlessly in our attempt to find our anticipated destination. We start businesses that are look-alike to whatever is already successful, or we fail to truly examine the value already present in our raw materials.

Since it is unlikely that we will ever have a crystal-clear path, that we will ever understand the necessary steps to achieve immediate success out of the gate, I have been on a life-long quest. I have been searching to find the levers we can grab to affect our desired outcomes. Once I started to read about the alchemist's lore of the past (as practiced by the Merlin's of Arthurian legend and folklore) I started to understand what they were looking for.

Alchemists did not create gold for wealth, though certainly wealth would be a byproduct of their mastery, but rather for transformation. The ability to choose the next step in any endeavor and transform from where we are to where we choose to be.

I didn't experience a sudden epiphany, after which everything became clear as day, following that first Economics class at UCLA. I didn't receive a flash of insight informing me that alchemy was going to provide a pathway that could illuminate a way to effect change. All of those ideas took time to coalesce in my mind. But what did happen from that first day at UCLA was that I was given explicit permission to become curious and chase the idea that we have agency over things that I had previously thought to be out of our control. That is what I got that first day. And that is what led me down a path that today has translated into taking old-school principles and turning them into a modern idea creation system.

2. WHY SYNAPTIC ALCHEMY?

Now that you have found yourself starting your alchemical journey, let's move forward into the process of moving an idea from a broad concept into a successful endeavor.

What the alchemical thinkers of the past and the modern thought leaders of the present understand is that the magic of alchemy is not in the actual turning of lead into gold. That's just the metaphor. The magic of alchemy is learning a repeatable process for moving an idea from a broad concept into a successful venture, whether in the form of a business, viral idea or social action.

The repeatable process is important. It is a process. Not a guarantee of success. All successful ideas walk the alchemical path and implement the alchemical transformation. However, just because you walk the path does not guarantee success. However, not walking the path does almost assuredly imply a harder journey.

That's why the subtitle of the book is "The Art & Science of Turning Ideas into Gold." The science part is that there is a predictable path that gives you an unfair advantage, no matter where you come from or what aspect of life you choose to apply it. The art part is that how you walk the path and navigate your journey from start to finish is not a predictable one.

The secret of turning ideas into gold can be seen in the clues left by prior Synaptic Alchemists. They demonstrate a step-by-step process that can be replicated in business, politics, social movements, entertainment, and fitness.

Synaptic Alchemy clues can be found in the Apple Macintosh computer or the new wave of automobiles like Tesla electric cars. Let's learn how to bottle those golden ideas and use them to fuel your own.

> "We choose to go to the Moon in this decade and do the other things, not because they are easy, but because they are hard;"
>
> — John F. Kennedy

Another Synaptic Alchemist, John F. Kennedy, passionately declared these 25 words on September 12, 1962; and created a national movement that saw Kennedy's goal realized only seven years later in July 1969, with the successful Apollo 11 mission. It takes a Synaptic Alchemist to put a man on the moon.

Transforming ideas from concept to reality, is the key to innovation, success, and moving forward in any endeavor. Synaptic Alchemists reach for the stars and spin threads of gold wherever they look.

MODERN DAY BUSINESS

When you think of alchemy you might associate the idea with basic chemistry or the idea of seeking immortality that has followed the concept throughout the ages in addition to the common concept of turning lead into gold. You will be pulling back the curtain to apply a modern synaptic twist to alchemical process and apply it to your world in business, entrepreneurship, innovation and leadership.

Your alchemical mindset requires you to:

Think Intentionally & Act Decisively

Synaptic Alchemy represents this critical mindset. You've likely heard sports catchphrases being applied to business many times before. One famous catchphrase is hockey legend Wayne Gretzky's quote: "skate to where the puck is going," (actually stated by Wayne's father Walter Gretzky[14], to a young Wayne). That phrase has been used countless times in a business context.

There's nothing wrong with the phrase. In fact, it helps remind us to stay ahead of the markets and customer demand.

The process of alchemy is also a catchphrase that can be used in other areas. As you'll see in the alchemical process, when I speak of Nigredo, the blackening, I'm not actually encouraging you to burn something physical to the ground. I'm using the phrase: "burn something to the ground" to metaphorically link to the idea of letting go of traditional ideas.

This occurs from sports aphorisms to business and in many other contexts. Usually all you get is a simple statement that is supposed to remind you of a truth.

In Synaptic Alchemy, I'm going to present you with more than just a catchphrase or aphorism. I'm going to go deep into the step-by-step processes that alchemists of the past used in their quest for gold.

The study of alchemy historically was serious business. With roots that go back thousands of years, it is no surprise that the experimentation prompted by the alchemical process eventually led to alchemy becoming a precursor to chemistry[15]. 17th century scientist Robert Boyle (best known for Boyle's Law[16]) took an interest in alchemy, evidenced by his search for the Philosopher's Stone, while Isaac Newton, discoverer of the laws of gravitation and co-developer of calculus, was actively involved in alchemy to tease out the chemical makeup of the world.

For our purposes, the actual discovery of a method to turn lead into gold is not what the core of alchemy is all about. The core of alchemy is all about the transformation of something of little value into something of tremendous value. This is why alchemy is so significant in today's information age, where step-by-step conceptualization is essential to value creation.

This modern version of alchemy, where ideas are transformed into trends and products, is the foundation of the global economy, and political and socio-economic movements. It is this transformation process where all the value comes into existence as an idea morphs from concept to reality inside the crucible of the alchemical transformation process.

When Sergey Brin and Larry Page were coming up with Google, all they had was an idea about this thing called the internet and how it could be categorized. I posit that all of the value of Google came about as they morphed that simple idea into a physical artifact (computer code) and continued that transformation from simple code into a formidable machine to continue expanding on that idea.

Clearly a ton of work went into scaling that idea to the powerhouse that is now Google. But the alchemy of converting the synaptic storm of automating internet search into artifacts and a broad-based movement is where ALL the value was created.

It can be compared to creating diamonds. The raw materials are in the ground. Combining those raw materials with heat, pressure and time IS the alchemical process that turns carbon into precious gems. Of course, you have to mine the diamonds out of the ground, cut them, polish them, and fashion them into jewelry and get them into stores to sell. I'm not taking away any of the value that is added in those steps. But the transformation from carbon into precious gems is what we are after. It is analogous to what Google accomplished with ideas and it is how we will apply the concept of alchemy to the modern business world.

THE TRANSFORMATION

When we are looking to craft an idea into reality, to imprint a concept that has not previously existed on the ground, a transformation begins with the creator, founder, or progenitor of the idea, and continues to the audience or consumers of the idea.

At some point, the alchemical process produces artifacts that exist in the physical or virtual world. The transformation from an interesting idea into a new way of doing something is the alchemical process in its purest form. Although we may not think we are turning lead into gold when we are converting an idea into something that will change the way we interact with the world, that IS alchemy in action. The transformation itself, usually referred to as an alchemical process, has a set of steps that, if followed, provide you with a framework for completing the transformation.

When it comes to this transformation in modern day terms, there are many different places in which an alchemical process can take place.

- **Entrepreneurship** - The startup mindset, specifically around the development of new products that have the potential to upend existing industries or patterns, is an area that not only lends itself to Synaptic Alchemy, but in fact requires alchemy to grow. Synaptic Alchemy is not just about having a good idea. Let's be honest. Ideas themselves are a dime a dozen. The synaptic part is easy to come by. Just ask any entrepreneur about their ideas and you'll be bombarded with a flood of synaptic nectar. It is the conversion of these ideas into businesses that uses the alchemical process. All entrepreneurs who aren't just big talkers will need some type of alchemy.

- **Innovation** - The product development and creation process typically has massive failure rates. There are studies that show 85%+ of product innovations fail. Why is this the case? Product development is staffed with the best and brightest organizations have. So why is there such a high failure rate? I posit that new product development should follow an alchemical process, and that traditional product innovation completely ignores the steps of transformation. By following that process, step-by-step innovation can drastically increase success rates.

- **Leadership** - The alchemical process, and specifically Synaptic Alchemy, can be applied not only to ideas and products, but it can also be applied to how we lead and grow our ecosystem of individuals. From leading a company to leading a team, alchemy can make all the difference. High performance teams always employ some type of transformation. As working with a team necessarily requires building synaptic bonds between individuals, the process of going from simply a group of people to a high-performance team IS the alchemical process.

- **Marketing** - Understanding the ecosystem of individuals who will turn your idea into a full force movement is the practice of marketing. A deep understanding of who will engage with your idea requires the transformation from an inner point of view to an external set of eyes, and sometimes many eyes. I posit that this transformational process is Synaptic Alchemy implemented in its most subtle yet valuable manner.

- **Branding** - When you are trying to truly understand how the ecosystem of consumers of your idea will perceive you and / or your company, feel about your idea and eventually embody the idea as if it were their own, you have to transform from where you are to where your ecosystem needs to be. Just as in marketing, there is an alchemical process for brand development: a process that requires you to transform the questions you used to ask yourself into intentional thoughts as to how your idea will be absorbed.

- **Organizational Growth** - Some organizations grow successfully, and some do not make the leap over the growth chasm. When groups and entire organizations transform from one size to another, whether that growth is spurred on by demand, large new customers, geographic expansion, technological positioning, or simply a much-needed change in focus, the transformation required to successfully leap from one incarnation to another fits squarely within the alchemical process.

The Stages of Alchemy

Alchemy is not magic. It is not voodoo or hocus pocus. Alchemy is a process. Alchemy has been described as the ability to transform the goods of the earth, the raw materials of the world, into high value finished products.

In the world of Synaptic Alchemy what does this process entail?

As mentioned in the *How to Use This Book* section, I've broken the journey to becoming a Synaptic Alchemist into two segments:

1) Know Yourself

2) The Alchemical Transformation

Knowing yourself is vital since we often make steps that we think are in alignment with who we are, only to find that they end up being truly inauthentic. Why does that matter? Because you won't generate your most transformative leaps if you are doing something inauthentic to yourself. And you'll need to be at your best to turn lead into gold.

Once you've attained an understanding of your core values, beliefs, and behaviors, it is time to tackle the core mission of transforming lead into gold. The transformation of the base metals of your ideas into the precious metal (gold) of tangible creation. This is the transformation that we are all looking for. To create something lustrous from our essential capacities.

In getting to know yourself through the eyes of alchemy, there are two ideas you will come to master and use on a daily basis. The first is the identification of your personal *Prima Materia,* and the second is accessing your *Philosopher's Stone* to turn base metals into precious metals, which is to say ideas into gold.

1.) Identifying Your Prima Materia - Alchemists use the term "Prima Materia," or first matter, to identify the most basic materials or starting materials necessary for an alchemical transformation. Prima Materia could be considered the original material of the universe or simply the primitive formless base of matter. In Synaptic Alchemy, we are going to apply how you see the world through your *ideas, thoughts, concepts, and personality* as your Prima Materia, since they are essentially formless. It is the "Synaptic" part of Synaptic Alchemy.

The alchemy part comes in by taking the elements that make up your Prima Materia (your thoughts, ideas, hopes, dreams, personal paradigm, personality), and converting them into a Philosopher's Stone. These are core concepts of Synaptic Alchemy.

2.) Creating Your Philosopher's Stone - Yes, I know that this is a metaphor. You and I are not about to go on a Grail Quest to uncover or physically create the Philosopher's Stone. A simple understanding of the Philosopher's Stone is that it is a substance that can turn low value inputs (such as lead) into high value outputs (such as gold). In Synaptic Alchemy, the Philosopher's stone is fashioned by the process of fine tuning your *capabilities*, so that they catalyze your transformations.

Your Philosopher's Stone is how you externally interact with the world; asking the right questions; driving your executed intention.

We'll spend a good chunk of time working through how to convert formless ideas into a fine-tuned process, and how this in turn creates your own personal Philosopher's Stone. It is the deep understanding of your personal fundamental forces and how those forces can be harnessed to create massive transformations that is at the heart of Synaptic Alchemy.

THE ALCHEMICAL TRANSFORMATION

Once you have solidified your Prima Materia and crafted your Philosopher's stone, you now need to start turning lead into gold, turning low-value inputs into high-value outputs. So, what are your inputs? Your base materials? You can think of them as your ideas. They can be formless (think Google's search terms) or they can be physical materials such as wood, steel, and concrete.

In this book, we will be focusing on the formless base materials that come from your mind. These formless factors (like your ideas) will eventually impact and create physical goods. But the first and most important transformation is the transformation of your mindset.

A Modern Point of View

Understanding the alchemical process itself as it was conceived and honed over the centuries can be a challenge. Alchemy has its own language, its own set of terms, concepts and principles. I am pretty sure that the vast majority of the readers of this book are not interested in a complete A-Z course on alchemy, the history of alchemy, or becoming experts in chemistry or other related fields.

Synaptic Alchemy is designed to take core principles and create a pathway: to transform fuzzy ideas into something valuable and tangible. There are primary ancient concepts from alchemy that can be adapted to business and the modern world. Although there are many texts on alchemy, the common thread between them centers on achieving a transformation, regardless of how the story of transformation is written.

We are going to take the story of alchemical transformation and apply it to ideas and business. **We will explore alchemy through the lens of business, modern ideas, and innovation.** This perspective allows us to shift our point of view to a set of concepts that we can use to transform ideas into movements, ideas into flourishing businesses, or ideas into public policy. Synaptic Alchemy provides a framework that will help you to design and execute a formal and repeatable process or foundation for innovation across startups, leadership and large organizations alike.

Synaptic Alchemy is my version of traditional alchemy. I have used these tools, skills, and mindsets time and again in many aspects of my life. I know that if you apply them properly, they can work for you too.

There will be times that I may veer away from tradition or ancient history or the complexities of a paradigm that has had its own growth and maturity over the years. But these detours are in service to applying the concepts to modern thinking and specifically to innovation and the building of ideas, whether for business purposes or otherwise.

This gets a bit complicated, but I promise to boil it all down to a simple step-by-step process, so stay with me. Understanding the stages of the alchemical transformation will give you a deeper understanding of what you are doing at each stage and why you are doing a certain task.

Once you understand these stages, you can apply them to your ideas, social endeavors and businesses. That will really feel like magic. Taking the knowledge of the old masters and applying it to the modern world offers the potential of sparking a flash of insight that brings your concepts to life.

You will notice there is a significant overlap between Synaptic Alchemy and processes championed by traditional innovation thought leaders. In fact, there is significant overlap between Synaptic Alchemy and the Customer Adoption Lifecycle as presented by Geoffrey Moore in "Crossing the Chasm". This is not only intentional but by design. Innovation and customer adoption, which leads to widespread acceptance of change, are additional representations of the alchemical process.

You'll see references to academic and field work on innovation and customer adoption throughout the book, as many of the modern-day core concepts underlying these processes directly align with Synaptic Alchemy. This does not diminish the power of the alchemical process nor diminish the power of modern models. In fact, the synergy between them strengthens these different paths as they all share a core foundation.

THE THREE STEPS

There are three big picture steps that you will put every single idea you have through in order to determine if an idea has the potential to become lustrous gold:

1. **Nigredo** - The destruction - This is when we stop thinking about things in their current way. This is when doing things in the same old way is disrupted.

2. **Albedo** - The re-birth - A new way of doing things emerges and blossoms. This new way of doing things has not become the standard yet, but a new way is possible.

3. **Rubedo** - The standardization - The new way becomes *the* way that everyone does things. This new way becomes the standard.

Understanding how to put ideas and concepts into the three alchemical stages is vital and will require you to apply Intentional Thinking at each stage. Applying the alchemical process to your idea can provide you with the path needed to move from lead to gold, from idea to movement, from concept to successful product. We will take a deep dive into each of these areas and break down how each stage can be used to handcraft the next evolution of yourself, your company, and your ideas.

3. PERSONAL ALCHEMICAL EXPLORATION

It is vital that you know how you think, what your internal decision-making processes are, and how those processes manifest themselves in the real world. This is what the next section is all about. Your first step into the alchemical journey, and your first moments of knowing who you are as a Synaptic Alchemist.

The following section presents a pathway to uncovering these deep personal aspects that form the core of who you are. Then we explore how you can best use these aspects in your journey. It may sound simple, but it is not easy.

Truly knowing your inner self, how you see the world, constitutes your core ability to make transformations. Alignment between your core abilities and the transformations you are attempting is invaluable to the alchemical process.

KNOW THYSELF

Knowing who you are and how you see the world is crucial to the practice of Synaptic Alchemy. This is because who you are, how your synapses fire, and what triggers your innermost understanding of the world is the foundation for turning ideas into gold. There is an Ancient Greek aphorism, "know thyself", that was inscribed at the Temple of Apollo at Delphi. The saying has woven its way throughout history from the ancient Greek play "Prometheus Bound" to Socrates in his history titled: "Memorabilia."

> "To know thyself is the beginning of wisdom."
>
> —Socrates

Knowing who you are at your most cellular level will be vital in your alchemical journey.

Image 3 - The Temple of Apollo at Delphi

A wonderful expression of knowing thyself comes from Chip Conley. He is a seasoned entrepreneur and New York Times bestselling author of "Peak: How Great Companies Get their Mojo from Maslow"[17]. Chip founded Joie de Vivre, one of the largest boutique hotel companies in the world, and was its CEO for 24 years. Afterwards, he went on to work with Airbnb, as their Global Head of Hospitality, guiding them to build their team and culture in one of Airbnb's fastest growing periods.

Being able to change an industry, twice no less, with Joie de Vivre significantly contributing to creating the boutique hotel market and Airbnb establishing the new online rental marketplace, in essence a hotel without hotel rooms, Chip definitely fits the role of entrepreneur extraordinaire.

I am sure that Chip sees himself as an entrepreneur, however, he calls himself a Social Alchemist, and that is definitely his true calling. Growing businesses is the vehicle he uses to express himself. Chip truly knows himself in that as a Social Alchemist he brings people together via unique experiences and handcrafts a way for them to belong and connect.

It is this deep understanding of himself, of knowing his true essence and how that essence is expressed on the ground in real life, that is the success mixture allowing him to ignite ideas and IS a prime example of knowing thyself.

This is not to say that you discover your inner core traits just once in your life. You will evolve. You will grow. You will change. You will have to discover and re-discover yourself continuously as time goes on. When and how you choose to take this journey of discovery is up to you. But if you are to turn any idea into gold, at some point you will come face-to-face with the person in the mirror and have to introduce yourself.

Taking the time and following a process to uncover your inner traits is what the first segment of Synaptic Alchemy is all about. Knowing your alchemist type and knowing how you express that type in the world corresponds to two ancient processes:

- Prima Materia - Know what type of alchemist you are.

- The Philosopher's Stone - Know how that type is expressed.

These are core to becoming a Synaptic Alchemist and will reveal the traits you use to understand and transform the world.

YOUR PRIMARY MATTER

"He who knows others is wise; he who knows
himself is enlightened"

—Lao Tzu

Alchemists believe there is a starting material or essence
that is almost impossible to capture in words or to describe how
to put into use; it is known as the mother of all elements. The
job of an alchemist is to capture this. They call this essence
Prima Materia or primary matter. How does this apply to us in
the modern day as a tool to help us succeed in life?

What is your Prima Materia?

Primary matter that expresses its essence in ancient
alchemy, and practically in how you see the world, is the starting
ingredient for your journey. For the entrepreneur, the innovator
or the creative deconstructionist, it consists of your core

personal traits. It is your raw persona and the perceptual filter through which you view inputs from the external world.

Discovering your Prima Materia is sort of like trying to pin down your shadow. This is because your Prima Materia is the essence of you: something akin to your soul or spirit. However, that doesn't mean that you can't gain an understanding of your Primary Matter. You get to glimpse your Prima Materia through your personality. The practice to Know Thyself is a critical tool in the journey of understanding and embracing alchemical power.

You are going to see the term personality used as a reference for your Prima Materia throughout this manuscript. That is because you can see and understand your personality, which is just a reflection of your amorphous Prima Materia.

Growing up, I really didn't understand my own personality. I knew as much—which is to say as little—as every other teenager knew. I knew what I liked and what I didn't. But I didn't really understand how my personality was driving me to understand the world.

I've always been analytical and thought about the world in terms of bits and pieces or as systems. Even as a kid I wanted to know how things worked and how one piece affected all the other pieces and created an entire system. I would take apart

TVs and electronics in a search for what made them tick. I didn't want to know what each individual part did, I wanted to see the whole system in action and understand how it was put together.

That's my core Prima Materia expressed through my personality. My inclination to wonder, "hey, how do all these parts work together?" It is just how I see the world. Musicians see the world through music, writers see the world through words, I see the world through systems; how things are put together. We all have unique ways of understanding the world around us. That's Prima Materia at its core.

I believe it is my Prima Materia that drew me to computers, software and programming in the first place. I was endlessly fascinated with computers, even though I didn't study them in school (I was a Biochemistry and then an Economics major); their inner mechanisms came naturally to me and I had a fundamental understanding of their bits and pieces. I was so thrilled with the way computer scientists saw the world that I just couldn't stand the thought of sitting in a class and slowly learning the subject, so I went about exploring the field myself.

Using a credit card because I didn't have the cash to pay for it outright, I bought one of the first IBM computers that came out, and just started to learn. I picked up books on programming. YouTube was 20+ years away so I had to read technical manuals. I read magazines at school and I sat at the keyboard and banged out keystrokes until my eyes bled. Then I would dream about how those computers were thinking. I dreamt about how computer scientists were coming up with all sorts of ways to change the world.

Floppy disks, IBM computers, the Apple II or the Motorola 6502 processor were all terribly interesting to me in high school and when I just started college. But why? Why were they interesting to me? Because I had a vision of what the future held? Not really. I was still a teenager and I wish I was that prescient. But somehow, they fed a core hunger of mine to put the world into a structure that I could understand. Part of my Prima Materia is related to understanding the structure of systems. I was instantly aligned with the curiosity of "hey, how does part A affect part B and move part C?" and then was compelled to find an answer.

I was expressing my Prima Materia and I didn't even know it. Of course, being 16 years old at the time didn't give me much of a conceptual base to even know that Prima Materia existed, but that's what I was doing. I was taking my primary way of seeing the world and expressing it with the tools available at the time. Books, computers, chips and parts glittered with unlocked potential.

The problem with being 16 and fascinated with computers is that I had no clue what I was doing nor why I was doing it. I just knew that computers were interesting. If I knew then what I know now, I could have understood how to supercharge my way of thinking. But the problem is, bringing your way of thinking, your Prima Materia, to the point where you can see what is going on has two problems:

1.) Prima Materia is locked inside your head

2.) Prima Materia is amorphous

All Locked Up

With Prima Materia locked inside your head, you don't actually get to see it directly as you interact with the world on a day-to-day basis. We all have ideas in our head about how we operate in the world and we *think* we know how we think. It is kind of like thinking our reflection in the mirror is how we display ourselves to the outside world. Until, that is, you see yourself on video doing something and you are aghast at what you are seeing. Have you ever had a video taken of you doing something and been surprised? I've seen it done for golfers, football teams, athletes of all kinds, actors, and professional speakers, and unless you are used to it, the first time you see yourself it will probably be a jarring experience. You think, "is that how I really act?" Seeing yourself through the eyes of others, or through the unforgiving eyes of the camera, gives you a glimpse into yourself. Which is the same thing you need to do to really get a glimpse into your Prima Materia: holding a mirror to see into the depths of your personality.

How your personality, your Prima Materia, actually materializes in everyday life gives you insights into the stories that you are telling yourself; insights into the mindset that guides your actions and decisions every single day. Because we only get glimpses of who we truly are at times, what you think you know about yourself, and how you show yourself to the world, may be two very different things.

Think of it this way. It is similar to how hearing your voice on a recording sounds completely different than when you hear your voice in your own head in daily speech. That strangeness and resistance to hearing our own voice on a recording actually has a name: voice confrontation.

The typical explanation of voice confrontation is that when you hear yourself in daily conversation you hear both the sound that is transferred through the air as well as the sound that is transferred through your bones. The bone conduction itself provides low frequencies that are not part of how your voice is transmitted through the air.

Your voice sounds higher when it is recorded or when you converse with others than when you hear it directly yourself.

But that is just a difference in pitch, and not such a difficult issue to manage. That's the easy part about hearing yourself recorded. The easy part is that your voice might sound higher.

There is another part that is much more shocking. The real issue, and the real reason, we are put off by hearing our own voice in recordings is as follows:

There is a mismatch between our expectations of who we *think* we are and the outward experience of who we ACTUALLY are.

This is the core of it. If who we think we are is mismatched when it comes to how we see ourselves in the outside world then we will bristle at what we are seeing, hearing or experiencing. When it comes to our voices, our internal expectations do not always match who we present in recordings.

This is the same type of pressure you can experience when it comes to your Prima Materia. A mismatch between who you think you are, or who you wish you were and want to be, and how the rest of the world sees you, calls for some of self-exploration. We could label this internal and external personality mismatch "personality confrontation."

In essence, this means we have to confront our personality and see it as how the outside world sees it, and not as how we wish we were.

Why is it that making a commitment to knowing yourself, knowing your personality, and truly knowing how you understand the world is vital to the alchemical journey? Because, after all, your Prima Materia, your personality, is the starting place for all transformations. You had better know where you are starting from or you won't get very far.

There is an even more striking revelation when it comes to confrontation (both voice and personality) as we're defining it here. Experiments conducted in 1966 by psychologists Phil Holzemann and Clyde Rousey provide insights into voice confrontation beyond mere frequency mismatch or beyond the fact that your voice might sound a little higher when recorded. They concluded that hearing your voice disembodied from your speaking reveals extra-linguistic aspects of your personality, such as anxiety level, indecision, and anger.

This directly translates to personality confrontation. As you start to dig into your personality and mine your Prima Materia, you'll discover aspects you weren't aware of before. These aspects can both create previously unknown value and be ratcheted down when they do not serve you. It ultimately comes down to getting up close and personal with who you really are, with what your Prima Materia represents, and not just swallowing an idea of who you WANT to be. That's tough. It's tough for everyone.

There have been plenty of times in both my personal as well as my professional life when I had a serious confrontation with the man in the mirror. When my personality as an expression of my Prima Materia stood straight up and smacked me square in the face, showing me who I really was vs. who I wanted to be.

Wall Street

When I was finishing up my MBA, I had the idea that I would immediately go to Wall Street and work in finance. The classic move was to go into investment banking or trading. I had an image of working at Goldman Sachs or one of the other highbrow investment banks in New York, running big IPOs for the eBays and Amazons of the world. But working on Wall Street is not what my personality is all about and consequently is out of alignment with my Prima Materia. And I got a pretty good smackdown from a few of the closest friends I made while at business school. The conversation went something like this:

Me: "I'm going to go work for a top-tier investment bank."

Them: "Nope, you're going to get fired from a top-tier investment bank."

What? What were they saying? Didn't they see that high finance was something I had always wanted to do? They saw what I could not see. That it was something my ego always wanted to do. My friends basically said, "you're not cut out for the hierarchy of finance. You're going to tell someone off up the chain from you and you'll get fired." Ouch. That stung. I was indignant about their comments. Didn't they understand the direction I wanted to go and my capabilities? Clearly, they understood much more than I did. They saw my Prima Materia clear as day. I was meant to be an entrepreneur. What I wanted to see was something completely off-kilter from who I really was.

It took me a while, but I later realized that what my friends had seen was a much clearer picture of my personality/Prima Materia. I saw what I wanted to see at that time. That personality confrontation with my ego took a while to get into my bones. But once I let go of what I wanted to see, I was finally able to realize they were absolutely right. Going to Wall Street would have been disastrous for me. My true Prima Materia and how I expressed it through my personality and what Wall Street needs are two completely different things. Yep,

I would have gotten fired, maybe a bunch of times. It would have been a disaster for both Wall Street and me.

I was back to being an entrepreneur, which is exactly where I belonged, as it reflected a more accurate alignment with my personality as an expression of my Prima Materia. Alas, these lessons don't seem to stick the first time. Not recognizing the full impact of how strongly my own personality drove my behaviors caused me to get smacked down a bunch of times when I started my own company as well.

Entrepreneurship

It became abundantly clear in my last company that I was going to have a bunch of knock-down drag-out fights with my core Prima Materia and what I thought was my personality. When I started the company, I didn't realize the depth to which my personality affected my decision making. We all think we know ourselves, but unless you have made a deep personal exploration, you probably know yourself less than you think you do, at least I certainly did. As the founder of a startup, my decision making dripped its way down through the organization. Since I was unconscious of my decision process, this disconnect caused no end of stress to my team.

I'm all about seeing the next step, discovering the big picture, and pushing my team to do that as well. Once we have the big picture in mind, my personality—which is just the expression of my Prima Materia—quickly tires of spending a great deal of time with the details of implementation.

It took quite some time, a bunch of bumping heads with clients and employees, and eventually having the insights of outside counsel to get me to realize how I operate. To get me to realize how I was unconscious of how my personality, my Prima Materia, was affecting the team.

My core Prima Materia is reflected in how I operate with the world: through Big Pictures and Big Ideas. I often don't place enough emphasis on the details of implementation. Of course, this is great when I'm trying out new untested ideas or exploring how to expand into a new market, but it is not so great when it comes to implementing the details that are necessary to actually get things completed.

Many of my customers did not appreciate this part of my personality. My customers were looking for security and consistency rather than new revolutionary ideas. This directly impacted my ability to understand my customers and the market. It directly impacted my ability to grow the business. Not knowing how to leverage my Prima Materia with other necessary traits became a significant learning experience.

That learning experience culminated in a transformation in my last company. Instead of individuals running with ideas, we formed Productive Pairs, where two people of differing personalities—differing Prima Materia—would team up. This meant that my big picture personality would team up with a detail-oriented personality so we could not only come up with new ideas, but get them done in a timely fashion. It wasn't just a simple flip of a switch. Our Productive Pairing took effort and discipline. What came out of it was the benefit of combining our individual Prima Materia with the Prima Materia of others for the benefit of the team. And for me personally to realize what my Prima Materia was made of and to fully embrace it, bumps and all.

It's Gooey

The second piece of identifying your Prima Materia is to realize that it isn't solid. It is amorphous. It feels like smoke at times and can be difficult to capture. In reality, you never really capture your Prima Materia. You may see its reflection in the mirror, shadows on the wall, or perhaps a glimpse as it floats around the room. It is you, but it does not have substance. Your personality is ... well ... gooey. It is your way of seeing your world and the lens through which you make choices. It is your paradigm.

Your personality, your choices, what you pay attention to or stays in your field of vision, are controlled by your Prima Materia. HOW you make those choices, and WHY you make those choices, IS your Prima Materia. Your internal structure of decision making is the amorphous material you're working with.

This amorphous nature is what makes it difficult to grab hold of. However, the more you start to understand this amorphous gooey blob that is locked in your head, the more you will understand the unique measure of you as an alchemist.

In Synaptic Alchemy we consider the Prima Materia the synapses in your head themselves. The behaviors and personalities that you bring to bear on your world. It is your creative insights, the way you see the world, the questions you ask yourself, your mind's ability to willingly accept assumptions and the force of will you are willing to bring to bear to fashion your world.

YOUR PERSONAL
PRIMA MATERIA

Where do you hide your most precious qualities? That's the one motivating question you will need to answer when you are looking for your Personal Prima Materia. According to alchemical lore, the Prima Materia resides down deep in the bowels of your psyche, your synapses, and you are going to have to go there and dig around to find it.

If you are just starting your journey to becoming a Synaptic Alchemist, you may have never really thought about what brilliance lies in the hidden recesses of your mind. What is the primary matter that makes you unique and significant? Maybe it is the way in which you are always able to view the world from someone else's point of view? Maybe it is the questions you ask? Maybe it is the way you see the details of how everything works?

There are an infinite number of ways in which your personal concepts, ideas, and your paradigm, the way you see the world, can ignite a spark from the inside of your mind that affects the outside world. However, if you haven't been consciously exercising and looking for your Prima Materia, it may be hidden under a mountain of insecurities and personal limitations.

MY PERSONAL PRIMA MATERIA

I can draw on many stories that were affected by personal Prima Materia from my last company CID (Comprehensive Industrial Disability Management). The success of CID certainly wasn't a straight line. We zigged and zagged so many times that you would need an elevator to follow the ups and downs of the company's story. One of the zigs comes directly from my own personal growth and finding and embracing a certain aspect of my Prima Materia.

CID was a healthcare technology company started back in the recession of the early 2000's. Prior to starting CID, I didn't have any healthcare technology experience. I had some schooling in biology and had made a living in technology but was not formally trained in Computer Science (remember, my undergraduate degree is in Economics from UCLA). When CID was launching, I was starting a company with no knowledge of the industry and without an understanding of the language they spoke or the acronyms they used. There were many, many times in the early days that I had to ask for clarification or research what people around the table were talking about, just so I could be part of the conversation.

Initially, I was embarrassed and nervous about my lack of knowledge. Who wouldn't be? But holding on to those types of emotions is not my traditional modus operandi. So, I very quickly started to ask questions that no one would ask. Basically, because I did not carry the baggage of being in the industry for decades.

I quickly uncovered, polished, and fully owned a couple of my Prima Materia gems.

1. My ability to ask questions when I don't understand something without being embarrassed.

2. My ability to question why things are done in a certain way. Why they are being done at all. And what would happen if we did it not just a little different, but completely rethought the game board.

Figuring out these parts of my personality, parts of the primary way in which I see the world, and then finally allowing myself to accept these traits as not just my own personal quirks, but as part of what makes me unique, and then seeing their value in creating a company in an industry, is what let me understand that these are gems worth polishing: Prima Materia Gems.

Uncovering and polishing yours will be vital in your path as a Synaptic Alchemist.

Being conscious that you have unique strengths in your personality, that the way you see the world IS your Prima

Materia and that you can polish and use those gems to express the one-of-a-kindness that is you, is the first step towards augmenting the traits exclusive to expressing your inner alchemist.

One of the first questions that comes to mind is "How?" How do I become conscious of something that is not only locked up in my head but is amorphous as well? Sounds like it could be pretty complicated, and when we are confronted with something that is complicated we are prone to shying away and getting distracted.

Getting your hands on and understanding your Prima Materia requires the same process that astronomers use to understand some of the most fundamental bodies in our universe: Black Holes. Astronomers don't measure or view these astronomical phenomena directly. They look at them from an oblique point of view. They look at them from the side and not directly, through indirect observation. They understand how these powerful entities of the universe behave by seeing how they affect the universe around them.

That's exactly what we are going to do to get a handle on your Prima Materia. Instead of trying to understand something as complicated and ethereal as your personality directly, let's take a look at how it affects different areas of your life by exploring what you think is important, what you question, and how the beliefs you hold color the way you see the world.

YOUR PERSONALITY
AS EXPRESSION

Your personality is a great oblique way to get an understanding of your Prima Materia. Why? Because your personality is an outward expression of your inner thoughts and beliefs. Your personality is literally an outward expression of the inner you.

There are batteries of different personality profiles out there. Some you may have heard of and some might be brand new to you.

* DiSC assessment - Provides you with four domains: Dominance, Influence, Steadiness, Conscientiousness. Each of these domains gives you an understanding of how you can better understand yourself and adapt your behaviors to other people.

* Myers Briggs Type Indicator - Provides a direction of how you lean towards two different tendencies along four

domains: "Extraversion vs. Introversion," "Intuition vs. Sensing," "Thinking vs. Feeling," and "Judging vs. Perceiving." According to CPI, the test's publisher, 89 of the Fortune 100 companies use this test before hiring.

* Big Five - This model provides insights on five different traits in what is referred to as OCEAN. The traits are Openness, Conscientiousness, Extraversion, Agreeableness, Neuroticism. This model has demonstrated the most scientifically accurate magnitude of predictive correlations. This means that there is a significant connection between the information provided by the Big 5 with regard to your personality and how your personality is expressed in your behaviors.

It is essential that you understand what is inside of your head, or you will do things that just seem strange when you are moving towards becoming an alchemist. The Big Five give you some clarity on where your mind goes and how your personality reacts in certain situations.

The Big Five is the personality profile that we use inside Synaptic Alchemy. It is the profile that provides the most unique insights.

As an alchemist, you owe it to yourself to take the Big Five personality profile, really examine the results and start using it as a map to understand your day-to-day behaviors.

Rick Foster is one of the authors of "How We Choose To Be Happy[18]" (read this book with the insights below and you will experience the same epiphany I felt) and a brilliant Synaptic Alchemist in his own right. His deep understanding of how your personality is an expression of your Prima Materia, changed the way I interact both personally as well as professionally.

His book on happiness has a hidden epiphany. When researching his book on happiness, he didn't assume he knew what happiness was or that he could find a prescription for happiness from some academic literature; he literally reverse engineered it. He spoke to people who either self-identified as happy or were recognized by their close contacts as extremely happy. During that research he discovered something. He discovered nine domains that happy people use to become and stay happy. These are not techniques they learned or tools they implemented; these are the nine ways they go about living their lives.

He uncovered a unique theory of personality, a unique peek into the shared beliefs, the shared Prima Materia of happy people. What is even more interesting than the shared beliefs of happy people is what my first few meetings with Rick revealed.

We met when we both had the same large company as a client. My company was providing software to the customer while Rick was coaching their executive team. I had heard about his executive coaching program throughout the company and finally had a chance to meet him face-to-face.

We spoke and I was fascinated by his research on happiness. Then he told me why a happiness expert was coaching an executive team at a large, NYSE-listed organization. Happy people have the same traits and live with the same domains (i.e. have common Prima Materia) as A players, as great employees. That connection—that a well-defined personality and the hunger for self-awareness led to happiness—resulted in not only happy people but also excellent executives.

That insight was so sharp that it has elevated countless executive teams. The insight that knowing and enhancing your Prima Materia is important personally as well as professionally is an important revelation to keep in mind as you develop your ability to access this aspect of yourself.

You're Not That Agreeable

I thought I knew my personality. I've done a ton of personality tests and used the results to help better understand not just myself but the people around me, from family members to people in the company to customers. I knew that I was open to new ideas, new experiences, and in fact crave pushing the envelope to come up with new ways of doing things. At the same time, I know that ensuring that I get the tactical day-to-day activities done is something that requires the application of strong focus. I am great at exploring big ideas and at the same time need to engage my focus to have the discipline of executing on the daily tasks.

However, what I didn't know until I really dove into the Big 5 (thank you, Professor Adam Grant for guiding me in this direction) was my Agreeableness. It's not as high as I thought it was, nor as high as I thought I would want it to be. I have been told on many occasions that I am one of the most collaborative executives around when it comes to building consensus and relationships. I've always been proud of that ability to connect with people and be easy going. But what I also realized is that, when I have an opinion about how something should work, I can get very attached to that opinion.

Wow, I never thought about that. That I'm opinionated. That took a while to consume. That ended up being a positive when I started to understand both myself and our company.

Not only was I opinionated, but so was the company. As a team we worked hard to come up with the best solution for our customers. We did all the analysis. Ran all the scenarios. Eventually we developed a really strong, well-researched idea of what was the best way to do things. That worked for some customers. But it didn't work for others who really wanted a custom approach to doing things (you will see this play out in the Albedo phase of the Alchemical Transformation).

That's when my personality both got in the way and at the same time gave the company a guiding principle to sail towards. You see, being agreeable (in this context I mean I would create custom solutions for customers) when we first started the company worked fine for a while. But it wouldn't allow us to scale. We'd end up building customization A for customer A, then customization B for customer B, then customization C for customer C and so on. Until it just got too complicated to onboard customers H, I, J though Z. That's when my personality kicked in (well, when I finally let my personality kick in) and my team and I figured out the best way to do things and stuck with it.

It was hard on some customers. But that's part of making important decisions. It's part of running a business. Deciding who you are going to work with and who you are not. Knowing who your customer isn't is just as important as knowing who your customer is.

Finally realizing that this is part of my personality, and that it is a good thing because we can focus where we work best, is what let us move forward at a fast clip.

If I would have tried to continue acting in a way that was not congruent with my Prima Materia, things would have gone in the wrong direction.

Working in alignment with your personality lets you express your Prima Materia, which is your core operating system and therefore constitutes your breakthrough strengths.

I remember working out of alignment with my Prima Materia. When I first started with computers, I found a way to land a large utility company as a client. My team and I were tasked with moving their existing computer system to the newest technology. And while I'm a skilled computer scientist, engineering is not the primary way I see the world. Consequently, when I'm working in an engineering mode, side-by-side with computer engineers, I'm not in a flow state.

You know what a flow state[19] is. It is that state where you execute effortlessly at the top of your game. Mihaly Csikszentmihalyi wrote about flow in his book "Flow: The Psychology of Optimal Experience."[20] When I'm in flow, I can see how the connections between all the pieces of the big picture fit together. That gives me vision as to how a system will work. World class software developers are in flow when crafting code as they see the world through an engineering frame of reference. Those two ways of seeing the world are completely different Prima Materia.

However, when you combine the big picture vision I express when I'm in flow with the step-by-step execution of good engineering, magic happens. The parts of the utility project when I was misaligned with my Prima Materia were slow and tedious. The parts when I was able to align my Prima Materia with my actions were smooth and ran effortlessly. Although at the time I didn't have the language to call what was happening a misalignment with my Prima Materia, I understand today how vital that alignment truly is.

YOUR PERSONAL COAT OF ARMS

Most of us have seen a coat of arms before. They are those wonderful symbolic representations that are used to establish identity[21]. The original coat of arms specifically established your identity on the battlefield in medieval Europe.

Image 4 - Royal Arms of the United Kingdom

Although the battlefields of medieval Europe are behind us now, codifying your identity in an easily recallable fashion is a uniquely important step in your alchemical evolution. Your Prima Materia (PM) can be ethereal and hard to capture. Sometimes we only get a glimpse of it through our personality, and even then, only obliquely through personality assessments. Consequently, creating your Prima Materia coat of arms will give you an identifier that you can quickly bring to mind when you are making decisions to ensure that your decisions are in alignment with your PM.

That is the exercise we are about to embark on. The creation of your own personal Prima Materia Coat of Arms

(PMCoA). Since many of us are not graphic artists, we're going to use language instead of images, and create a phrase that represents our coat of arms. That phrase will become an anchor so that you can quickly conjure up an image of your Prima Materia when you are making decisions. This will give you a lens to hold up to decisions so that you can ensure that the decisions you are making are in alignment with how you process the world.

That's a significant piece: The alignment of your Prima Materia and how you interact with the world. You can't be at the top of the alchemical game without your decisions and your inner direction being in alignment.

So, let's get started. Your PMCoA will be a three-word phrase that consists of an adjective, a noun, and a verb. Each word will have a specific relevance to your PM.

- Adjective: Your top motivation.

- Verb: The activity that feels most natural to you.

- Noun: How you fundamentally see the world.

We are not going to worry about perfect grammar at this point. In fact, the phrase that feels most authentic to you may be incorrect grammatically. The goal is to find a phrase, a coat of arms, that you can easily conjure up at a moment's notice.

Additionally, the words can come in any order that feels right to you. They don't have to be adjective to verb to noun. Maybe adjective then noun then verb feels best. Whatever works for you is what you should go with regardless of grammar since it is not a grammar exercise it is a personal reflection exercise.

You will probably go through several iterations as you come up with your PMCoA phrase. You'll find something that seems to fit, sleep on it for a couple of nights and then adjust as other ideas come to light. That's alright. In fact, that's the process that we are looking for.

It took a while, but currently my PMCoA is "Curious Systems Designer."

- The "Curious" piece (my adjective) is what moves me to action on a daily basis. It is what motivates me to act. I'm always curious about how things work, and that curiosity always has me asking questions about the inner workings of everything.

- The "Systems" piece (my noun) is core to my fundamental nature. It is how I see the world, as a collection of systems. As I find new puzzle pieces I almost "have to" see where those pieces fit in the puzzle and how they affect an overall system.

- The "Designer" piece (my verb) is the activity that feels most natural to me. I have a core drive to design new things as I start to understand the pieces. To design is the verb that I activate on a daily basis.

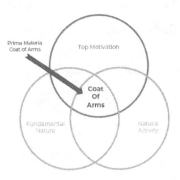

There are an endless number of three-word combinations that are possible for your coat of arms.

- Curious Systems Designer
- Graceful Movement Teacher
- Diligent Process Analyst
- Smart Exploring Musician
- Conscious Community Communicator

Those are all good examples of someone's PMCoA. Now it's your turn to create your own personal coat of arms. Follow along with the following simple exercise.

1.) Find your Top Motivation (adjective): Find an adjective that describes what motivates you to action in your day-to-day activities. Adjectives such as: curious, driven, stable, spiritual, gracious, skillful, motivated, joyful, honorable, loving, kind, empowering, dedicated, knowledgeable, versatile, peaceful, focused, fulfilled all are good places to start.

Think about a word that you would use to describe what you are like when you are getting really excited about something. A word that you would use when you are feeling that everything is flowing and time has stood still.

2.) Discover Your Natural Activity (verb): Really dig around for a word that describes what you tend to do—how you tend to behave—on a daily basis. Verbs such as: design, build, collect, explore, cherish, bounce, fly, grow, listen, contemplate, teach, think are good places to start.

Think about a word you would use to describe how you behave unconsciously when you encounter something new in the world. You can think of completing the sentence: "when I encounter something new I usually … it." That's not a perfect sentence and you'll have to adjust your grammar to get something to flow well with your phrase, but once you find the right word everything will become clear.

3.) Explore how you see the world (noun): Look for a word that describes the most basic level of how you view the world. Nouns such as: system, community, spirit, movement, melody, love, choice, finance, math, automation are good places to start.

Think about a word you would use to describe the most basic thing you look for when you examine the world. A word that would complete the sentence: "I see the world as ..." For example, musicians see the world through melody, music or notes. Writers see the world through words or phrases. Physicists see the world through particles or matter. That's the word you are looking for.

Don't think you have to get this right the first time. There is no right or wrong in this exercise. There are no common answers. This is designed to be personal to you. Try out different combinations. See which ones feel most natural. Take a few of your top combinations and try them on for a week. Go to work and use your coat of arms as your identification and see if it really is in alignment with your decisions. Once you find the right one, it'll stick pretty quickly.

Remember, at the beginning your coat of arms will change rapidly as you discard phrases that don't really fit you. But once you have a good fit, you'll quickly grow accustomed to it. Over time your coat of arms phrase may change, but it will be a slow evolution once you have a good fit.

4. THE PHILOSOPHER'S STONE

WHAT EXACTLY IS THE PHILOSOPHER'S STONE?

In traditional alchemical lore and history, the Philosopher's Stone is the substance that turns common metals like lead into the bright brilliance of precious metals like gold or silver. Because lore is just that, traditions and word of mouth knowledge, the lore of the Philosopher's Stone means it has several connotations. Turning lead into gold is just one. In the past, it was said that the Philosopher's Stone could enable its users to achieve immortality. Additionally, the psychologist Carl Jung has associated parts of alchemy with parts of the psychological journey, including individuation. The Philosopher's Stone has many interpretations. But, overall, it is an alchemical substance that presents as the catalyst for change.

Image 5 - Joseph Wright of Derby - The Alchemist

We will use the Philosopher's Stone in Synaptic Alchemy and our point of view of using alchemy as a framework for disruption, innovation and value creation in a unique context. The Philosopher's Stone will become a way that you express yourself to the world. THE Philosopher's Stone becomes YOUR Philosopher's Stone (PS for short) when looked at through the eyes of the Synaptic Alchemist.

We explored how your Prima Materia, your paradigm of the world and how it is expressed through your personality, is a guiding force in how you see things. Your Prima Materia answers the question "Who Am I?" That is the way in which you understand the world, take in the world. In Synaptic Alchemy, your Prima Materia is inward looking.

However, your Philosopher's Stone is the other side of that coin. It is the way you express yourself to the outside world. Your PS answers the questions of "How Do I Express Myself?" Or, in a more colloquial fashion: "Who Be I?" It is the way in which you interact with the world. It is expressive. Where Prima Materia is inward looking, your PS is outward looking. Your Prima Materia lets you bring things in, whereas your Philosopher's Stone lets you put things out.

WHAT DOES THE STONE LOOK LIKE?

> "What you most want to be found, will be found where
> you least want to look"
> —Professor Jordan Peterson paraphrasing
> Carl Jung "In sterquiliniis invenitur"

Since the Philosopher's Stone is the transformational substance that turns lead into gold, it will appear like magic. The magic that happens when you interact with this black-box substance is thrilling and enthralling. Since it feels like magic, we tend to search for it, rather than try and analyze it and make a new copy. Because who among us can copy magic? It is magic after all. You'll know the magic by experiencing its effects.

The PS is the magic that happens when:

- Ray Dalio, the legendary hedge fund manager, makes the right investment, at the right time, over and over again. It feels like lightning has been captured in a bottle.

- Internet retail giant Amazon amazes customers by having just the right product available at your fingertips for essentially instant delivery, transforming desire into satiation.

- Billy Beane, the legendary general manager of the Oakland A's baseball team, goes against the conventional wisdom of relying on scouting experience and intuition to build a team based on a statistical model, resulting in the A's achieving a record-breaking 20 consecutive wins.

Image 6 - Initial Google server stack at Stanford

- Google answers 2.4 trillion searches a year in less than 1/2 second on average per request.

- Apple provides connections to 1.4 billion iPhones with almost 5 Billion cell phones worldwide by all manufacturers which handle 23 billion text messages each day.

115

This is the power of the Philosopher's Stone when it comes to transformation. The transformation of raw materials into precious gems. This transformation feels like magic, because it essentially provides a magical new way of interacting with the world. Whether it is technology, medicine, or a political idea, the transformation can be truly awe inspiring.

Legend has it that the Labradorite gem embodies the PS. Labradorite is a mineral easily found in gem or crystal stores. Possessing a translucent sheen, the stone sparkles with green and blue hues crisscrossed with grey and black fissures and refracts iridescent flashes of light from its layers. The play of colors within the stone is known as labradorescence.

Image 7 - Labradorite Stone - Blue-Green color with Grey-Black Streaks

But why is the myth of the PS bound to this rock? It's the labradorescence. It is the iridescent flashes that appear to come from within the stone as if the stone is shimmering from an inner energy. It feels as if the stone itself has an inner light. It feels as if the iridescent flashes are mutating light in an extraordinary way. It feels as if it is the physical embodiment of a transformation. Other crystals shine and glimmer, but others seem to reflect the light in the room and provide a colored hue. Labradorite seems to glow on its own.

WHERE IS IT?

So where do you go looking for this legendary stone? Well, nowhere, really.

The PS is legendary for a simple reason. It doesn't really exist. There is no stone, no magic formula, no recipe, no crystal, no technology that embodies the PS, that embodies transformation. However, the real PS, not the legend, is much closer than you think.

It resides in you. Square in the center of the Synaptic Alchemist's chest.

The problem is you didn't know it was there until now. That's the next step. Finding your internal PS, gaining access to its power, and then activating that power in an intentional way.

Since you now know that a tangible PS is an illusion and that the real PS sits within you, we need to figure out what exactly that means.

We all have different ways of interacting with the world. We gather information and make models in our head about what the world is offering. Those models are important because we have to simplify the world so we can comprehend its complexity. That is your Prima Materia in action. Then, we have to think about how we are going to express ourselves. How that expression will be received and what is authentic in terms of how we see the world.

Your expression, the way you behave and express your personality, is, to the world, your Philosopher's Stone. Each of us is different in terms of how we express ourselves to the world. Some people are more aggressive. Some are quieter and more contemplative. Some might express by engaging in creation in all its forms, while others may explore the physical world through adventure and still someone else might delve into the inner workings of the universe.

While each of us is unique in our individual expression, there are some common patterns that have surfaced across cultures, timeframes and humanity in general, because we are all ... well ... human.

These common patterns of behavior or expression have been studied and analyzed and categorized into Archetypes.

Philosopher's Stone Archetypes

An archetype is a pattern of behavior, a way of thinking about the world, a specific set of universal traits and recognizable reactions. You are easily familiar with archetypes since they are common human characteristics that either you experience yourself or you've seen in others every single day. Once you understand someone's archetype, it becomes easier to relate to them without having to spend as much time pondering how they operate. An archetype is a big picture way of thinking. It is different from a stereotype, in that a stereotype is an oversimplification of a behavior pattern. A stereotype can be positive or negative, but it is simple (think "the jock"), where an archetype is rich and complex and nuanced (think "the creator"). An archetype represents a universal truth about how we express our humanity.

A number of different archetypes have been identified. In "The Hero of a Thousand Faces," Joseph Campbell demonstrated eight different archetypes in literature that have become common across cultures and time. Everything from the Hero to the Guardian to the Shadow. You've seen these archetypes expressed in tales from Star Wars to Lord of the Rings.

Carl Jung proposed 12 archetypes that exist within the human psyche. Of course, there is significant crossover between Jung and Campbell, given that Joseph Campbell was a serious student of Carl Jung's work. Included among Jung's archetypes are the Explorer, the Magician, the Outlaw and the Jester. "The Archetypes and the Collective Unconscious" is Jung's exploration of human behavior extrapolated into archetypes.

There are lists and lists of archetypes. From masculine and feminine to literary to psychological. However large or long a listing of archetypes is, they do us no good if they aren't actionable and make a difference when it comes to your alchemical journey.

For Synaptic Alchemy, we'll stay with Carl Jung's 12 archetypes. There is no need to reinvent the wheel and create another category of archetypes when Jung's work is so relevant and deep. However, we will put our own Synaptic Alchemy spin on the archetypes so that they fit within the context of Knowing Thyself.

When someone describes who they think you are, they really are describing your PS. This is because no one knows the internal you, how you process the world—that's your Prima Materia. However, they CAN see how you express yourself.

The Philosopher's Stone, in general, and your personal PS in particular, is the magic that can be used to transform lead into gold. Specifically, it transforms the inner you, your Prima Materia, to the outer you, your expression. That expression is what you will use when you go forward into the physical world and start finding chunks of lead and turning those chunks into bright shiny golden medallions.

The following describes the 12 Jungian archetypes with regard to how they relate to Synaptic Alchemy. Each archetype is a form of Philosopher's Stone; something each Alchemist carries around with them in their chest, in their spirit. Read through the summary of each archetype. You'll find one, or more, that speak to how you express yourself in the world.

We all express individual characteristics of many of the archetypes. For example, although my personal Philosopher's Stone Archetype is the Magician, I have significant elements of the Caretaker personality. I don't see the world through a

Caretaker lens (I see the world through the Magician's eyes) however, I do tend to take care of those around me. So, even though you may relate to some aspects of each archetype, as you sort through them you'll start to understand a primary way you express yourself.

Read the details until one primary archetype really speaks to you and how you express yourself. This is how you can start to sort through and find your PS. One archetype will really jump out at you and fit how you primarily interact with the world.

There Can Be Only One ... (Well Twelve)

Each of us, all alchemists, especially all Synaptic Alchemists, express a little bit of each archetype through our individual Philosopher's Stone. For example, you might notice that at times you express yourself as a Caretaker and then other times you definitely embody the Hero. The trick is in discovering your primary archetype, the one you express on a daily basis. The one that encapsulates the way you interact with the world each and every day. You will find that one archetype represents the primary way in which you express yourself the majority of the time.

There was a movie back in the '80's called Highlander. It featured an expression, "there can be only one," which was a reference to the movie plot that only one immortal could receive the Prize at the end of the movie: unfortunately, by beheading all the other immortals. This is kind of like your search for your primary Philosopher's Stone archetype, but without the violence. Although you may recognize aspects of your personality in each archetype, there will be Only One archetype that provides an overarching view of, well, you.

THE OUTLAW

"The loudest sound you hear will be your heart racing"

—Harley-Davidson

Summary: The Outlaw, AKA the Rebel, is all about shaking up the status quo and finding themselves by exploring outside of established norms. Thinking about disrupting the common patterns found in society and consequently changing society and moving it towards a better outcome, even if that outcome requires—in its fullest form—a revolution, is core to this PS. The intention and principles of the Outlaw are how they define their direction. Moving towards disrupting everyone because they don't notice there is a better way is the positive side of the Outlaw.

It is a delicate balance to be an Outlaw archetype and even more so to have an Outlaw Philosopher's Stone type. The

125

alchemist who possesses the Outlaw PS will have a desire to shake things up, to have agency and power over their circumstances by pushing on the boundaries of what is already accepted. This can create a very unique way of looking at the world. As long as the desire is to create better conditions for all involved, then the individual behind this expression of the Philosopher's Stone will be followed and hailed as a visionary.

Desire: The alchemist with the Outlaw Stone archetype is looking to disrupt the status quo in order to change things and move society forward. Being a rebel or a revolutionary is core to this PS. The stone's drive will be to see where the standard way of doing things trivializes people and makes them powerless. Finding a way to break that cycle is what motivates the Outlaw archetype. There are two phases to this cycle: Identifying situations that are keeping others powerless, and then finding a way to break those situations and release the pressure.

Being conscious of this drive to break the system is vital to this alchemist and this stone. A system may have come into existence to provide a common service to all, even though it may not be the best for any given individual it may have started with good intentions. However, the road to Hell can be paved with good intentions. Looking at the intentions of the desire to break a system is vital. Breaking a system must be done with an intention and a plan to create an alternative that is better for all than the current one. The drive to change the status quo is strong with this Stone archetype.

Example: Malcolm X is a pure example of the Outlaw. Most revolutionary figures at some point in their lives fit into this category. Malcolm's quote *"Nobody can give you freedom. Nobody can give you equality or justice or anything. If you're a man, you take it"* is in itself a call to the Outlaw archetype. His drive to change society in a way he saw as combatting injustice is core to the Outlaw Stone.

Changing society, or shaking up the status quo, does not have to be accomplished through force. Some of the most astonishing changes to the normal way of doing things have occurred when the change came without a frontal assault. The quote "It is amazing what you can accomplish if you let somebody else take the credit," (John Solbach) is a perfect example of how quiet persistence is often the best way to shake up the status quo.

Looking at the traditional way of doing things and figuring out where that can be broken apart is very appealing to this PS.

Behaviors: The Outlaw PS archetype typically has not achieved power or position by having it handed to them through traditional channels. This means that the standard game board of life is not where they have the most power. You will look at life as a set of rules to be broken to allow upward mobility for all. Instead of pushing up against the normal set of rules, you will look to figure out where the rules can be broken. That is why the motto of the Outlaw is "Rules are meant to be broken." However, just breaking rules because they can be broken can leave the Outlaw constantly protecting themselves from the establishment.

Alchemists possessing the Outlaw PS will think differently about this issue. They will look at the establishment and instead of trying to upend the entire game board, will attempt to see where making small changes in rules now will have a large impact later on. Changing the game from the inside out is the most effective mechanism for the Outlaw Stone, because you can dedicate all the resources typically reserved for protecting against the establishment to changing the rules of the game. And once you change the rules of the game, the entire system is upended without any resistance.

Expression: The Outlaw easily sees the brittle parts of a system and is driven to break them.

Language: "Rules are meant to be broken"

Darkest Fear: "Ending up powerless in a system ready for change"

THE MAGICIAN

Summary: Magicians strive to understand the basis of how the world works in order to mix that understanding with new ideas so they can cast a spell on the world. The spell is cast not via illusion or illusory steps but rather by transforming a common belief into a compelling future. If you feel a driving desire to understand how the world works at its most basic level and convert that knowledge into a promising future, then you will align with the Magician Stone archetype.

Desire: Magicians want to know how things work at their most fundamental level. They then take that knowledge and bring into being the most exquisite of worlds. They essentially are looking for secrets in order to cast a spell. Not a magical spell, but a spell grounded in understanding.

Really understanding what things are at the most basic level is at the core of the magician. The deep understanding of the underlying principles of how things work is what gives this archetype a sense of magic. The magician sees a vision and intuits the pathway to achieve that vision by understanding the basic parts of everything that vision is made of.

Example: Elon Musk is a textbook Magician innovator. He talks about "First Principles" thinking as the way he sees the world. He deconstructs the world into basic assumptions that cannot be reduced any further. That allows him to understand the basics of what to focus his attention on.

When Musk began looking into sending a rocket to Mars (what eventually became the spring point from which the aerospace company SpaceX was born), he encountered a major challenge. He discovered the cost of purchasing a rocket was incredibly high (up to $65 million). That high price forced him to start to rethink the problem.

"I tend to approach things from a physics framework," Musk said in an interview. "Physics teaches you to reason from first principles rather than by analogy. So, I said, okay, let's look at the first principles. What is a rocket made of? Aerospace-grade aluminum alloys, plus some titanium, copper, and carbon fiber. Then I asked, what is the value of those materials on the commodity market? It turned out that the materials cost of a rocket was around two percent of the typical price."[22]

Behaviors: Magicians are typically driven by the desire to gain knowledge of the outside world and are constantly on the hunt for new understanding through books, teachers, or education—whether that education is formal or informal. Constant learning and a constant drive to understand how and to deconstruct are hallmarks of the Magician archetype.

Expression: The magician expresses a vision for the future of the world that arises from the magic they learn about the true nature of things.

Language: "It can happen"

Darkest Fear: "Don't be cursed"

THE HERO

Summary: The Hero archetype is all about making the world a better place. You can think about the Braveheart movie character or first responders like the police, fire department, military service members or astronauts. The Hero could also be described as the warrior, rescuer, or elite athlete. It is not just about being courageous, but it is about inspiring others so everyone in our close circles and the world at large can be better. The Hero archetype is bold and strong not just for themselves, but also so that we can all become a little bit of a hero ourselves.

The motto of an alchemist who has the Hero Stone archetype is "where there's a will, there's a way." That provides a good glimpse into how this archetype will use their PS. A Hero always looks to find a way to win, no matter how much the odds are stacked against them. It is not just a craving to win that drives the Hero, but a craving to fine tune their skills to prepare for the eventual battles that will come their way.

When you have a Hero Stone archetype, being prepared for a battle or competition is not the only goal. Allowing others to view their prowess and thus make the world a better place overall because everyone rises up to the challenge is as primary a goal as any competition.

Helping those who legitimately cannot help themselves is core to an alchemist who holds this type of PS. But, because the Hero tends to be highly disciplined and focused, if others have the capacity to rise up and be Heroes on their own, the alchemist with the Hero PS will push them to put in the work to rise up.

Desire: The Hero has an immense desire to defend those who can't defend themselves and to engage wherever courage and bold actions will make a difference. Making a difference in the community is something that definitely rings true to the Hero. The desire to be on top is not just a competitive yardstick for the alchemist with this Philosopher's Stone. The desire to be on top, to win, to be in the lead position, is a desire to evolve the entire tribe.

You'll feel your Hero PS pull on you when you expect high standards of others. It is part of finding the will to succeed, and succeed in circumstances that are highly competitive and have significant consequences. You'll express the Stone through a desire to accomplish heroic and often Herculean tasks.

There is a secondary drive within the Hero archetype, and that is the drive for mastery and competency. The drive to master the skills that are important in competition, in the board room, in an emergency and on the battlefield. It is not mastering skills just for the sake of mastery. Rather, it is mastery for the sake of being more useful to others in need.

The drive for courage in the face of danger and mastery of the skills to succeed is key to this Stone archetype.

Example: Strong leaders and presidents certainly can hold the Hero Stone solidly in the palm of their hand. Think of John F. Kennedy, Teddy Roosevelt or Nelson Mandela as quintessential Heroes. These leaders were not just driven to succeed on their own, they were driven to empower and inspire others to succeed and rise to the challenge as well.

If you think of JFK's famous "We choose to go to the Moon" speech at Rice University in 1962, you precisely hear his Hero's Stone archetype in action.

"We choose to go to the Moon in this decade and do the other things, not because they are easy, but because they are hard; because that goal will serve to organize and measure the best of our energies and skills, because that challenge is one that we are willing to accept, one we are unwilling to postpone, and one we intend to win, and the others, too."

—John F. Kennedy

JFK is inspiring his entire tribe, which at that point is the entire population of the United States, to do something hard. To use the skills necessary to win, and to not back down. That is almost a textbook description of a Hero archetype.

Nelson Mandela realized that as a leader, as the hero of his countrymen, he could have given into his base instincts and turned on the people that incarcerated him. But he realized that would lead his country into a civil war. Instead, he made a different choice. He heroically led his people by deciding that forgiveness was the ultimate path to raising up all of his countrymen, his tribe, to become the best version of themselves. That was a difficult and heroic task.

Behaviors: Looking for injustices that the Hero can address is almost automatic with this archetype. Keeping an eye out for teams and tribes with the highest quality standards and commitment to success to connect with and join is also imperative for this type of alchemist. This means that finding a team that can make a difference on a large scale is something that all alchemists who express this Philosopher's Stone are looking for. It is this search for excellence that burns bright.

Persevering against all odds is a stellar behavior expressed by the Hero Stone. Fred Smith, the founder of Federal Express, received a C in his economics course at Yale when he proposed a new kind of freight service. He persevered and spawned a $3-billion industry that didn't exist previously. He was born with a birth defect and had to walk with braces. He persevered and eventually was able to join the US Marines.

The perseverance against all odds, in fact, searching for a task to persevere through, is integral to the Hero and how they express their PS.

If you have the desire to fight the tough fight, protect those in need, expand your skills to become the best you can be, and persist when all others may quit, then the Hero Stone archetype will deeply resonate with you.

Expression: The Hero builds their arsenal to have the tools to win in a competitive field that will inspire everyone to become the best version of themselves.

Language: "Where there's a will, there's a way."

Darkest Fear: Being too weak or vulnerable to muster the resources necessary to vanquish the enemy.

THE LOVER

Summary: The Lover archetype is about connection, intimacy and the experience of falling in love. It is not just romantic love that the Lover Stone archetype craves, but the intensity and power of a unique bond. The hunger of the Lover to feel unique and special in the world creates a passion around not only feeling special but making every person in the world feel special as well. When you have a Lover's Stone archetype, not only is falling in love with falling in love a unique elixir, but falling in love with the pleasures of the senses is also quite enticing.

The ability of the Lover to connect deeply with the senses is vital. Everything can be enhanced through love and that includes the environment. A Lover archetype will desire a sensuous feeling around everything. This might include the lighting of their environment, the scent of their room, or the texture of the food at the table. The ability to become intimate, to bond, even with the smallest of items, is unique to this PS.

Desire: The Lover craves interactions with others, to show appreciation to others and to enjoy the experience of the senses. This desire to be accepted and deeply involved with the tribe, whether that tribe is a very close-knit family or a large extended community, is not of primary importance. Having a strong emotional connection to others is what drives this Stone archetype.

Being able to connect with others not only one-to-one, but making others feel completely connected even when the Lover may not know the other person is their primary drive. This PS is unique because they crave a deeply connected world where each person feels accepted. Building and enhancing the quality of the relationships around the world is key to this Stone archetype.

Example: Beyonce is the quintessential Lover archetype. She casts a spell not only by having her fans fall in love with her music, dancing and just pure expression, but also to enable her fans to have their tribe fall in love with them. Even Beyonce's music is all about the art of falling in, and staying in, love. Think about the lyrics to her song "Single Ladies," the main riff says, "If you liked it then you should've put a ring on it," which is a direct statement about falling in love and then deciding to commit to it.

It is not just that Beyonce crafts music that speaks to the heart—although that certainly is part of how she expresses herself to the world. It is that Beyonce's expression is all about the connection of her work to her fans through costume, set design, even the most intimate details of her life are expressed through her work. Think about her album "Lemonade." This was her second visual album where she told an intimate personal story, not just through popular music, but through the videos that were released as well. The visual story of this chapter in Beyonce's life was brought home to her tribe through the combination of music and visuals.

Beyonce's language also gives us a window into her use of the Lover Stone

"The most alluring thing a woman can have is confidence."

To bring the world close and be alluring to her tribe is a quintessential trait of the Lover.

"When you love and accept yourself, when you know who really cares about you…"

Knowing who in her tribe truly cares about her, and then giving that point of view to the others in her tribe, allows everyone to be loved.

Behaviors: Building a tightly bound tribe is essential to the Lover. You'll feel a desire to bond not just with your inner circle, but with those individuals close to you and then to expand that bonding to all the world. It is a wonderful desire to create a caring world. The way this desire is expressed is through connection activities. This includes creating tribes of like-minded people across large geographic boundaries. Think about the impulse to create different groups when those groups are physically separated. Using virtual tools to build strong communities. Organizing gatherings that are at large scale and can accommodate a great many but feel intimate in their connection. This is the language of the Lover archetype.

When the Lover is expressing, it feels like everyone is working on bonding. Creating physical spaces, virtual spaces, and intellectual spaces where it is safe for the tribe to be engaged is how this is expressed. When a group of strangers comes together in a company, the Lover will ensure that they feel cared for and have the room to express all of the uniqueness of their personality. This may be expressed as building teams and organizing those teams with suitable leaders and experiences.

If you have the desire to expand community and build cohesive tribes, then the Lover Stone archetype will deeply resonate with you.

Expression: The Lover expands communities and builds a world where every member feels accepted.

Language: "In this moment we are one"

Darkest Fear: "Being left alone and feeling unwanted"

THE JESTER

"Do your thing and don't care if they like it."

— Tina Fey

Summary: Tina Fey's quote really does present a full picture of the Jester. With the motto of "You only live once," the Jester archetype is all about fully living in the moment. That is a unique perspective, as it is very different from the majority of the other archetypes, and has a specific meaning to the alchemist who claims the Jester as their Philosopher's Stone. Whereas many of the other archetypes are focused on fine tuning their skills to turn lead into gold in the future, the alchemist who holds the Jester as their stone is focused on turning whatever is in front of them into gold. That's a very unique way of looking at the world.

Being able to stay in the moment gives the Jester a chance to be irreverent and to break conventional norms because this stone enables you to be truly unconcerned with others' opinions of you. That is why Jesters are able to speak truth to power and at times connect tribes who may feel like outcasts or cannot truly express themselves. The alchemist who applies the Jester gives voice to those whose voices may have been quieted, either by their own nervousness, or by command and control measures.

Desire: When you express yourself with a Jester stone, you are given the chance to see the world with a childlike wonder. Jesters are imbued with the gift of being exuberant and life affirming. That is a persistent craving: To explore life as play and trust that no matter what the circumstances, life will create a safe playground that lets everyone explore the joy of living in the moment.

Your joyous views are what imbue others with the ability to let loose and release some of the self-imposed constraints that many of us live with. Although expressing the Jester does not mean you need to be the life of the party every moment of every day (although many times that is just how Jesters express themselves on a consistent basis), it does mean always reminding your tribe there is more to life than fretting about the future or reminiscing about the past. It means reminding your tribe that this moment, and experiencing it as joy, is key to feeling fully alive.

Example: Traditionally individuals who become comedians are at the core of this archetype. It is not necessary for you to work in standup to express this archetype. However, there are many institutional constraints on individuals who don't work in comedy that make it difficult for them to express their inner Jester.

Jon Stewart is a wonderful example of a unique alchemist who expresses the Jester. Not only did Jon Stewart cut his teeth with stand-up comedy, but his unique sense of irreverent thought-provoking lines of inquiry on the Daily Show truly highlight how the Jester can take a taboo subject, or a subject that has been cloaked in convention, and break it open to make it accessible.

Stewart's quote on the Daily Show: "if you watch the news and don't like it, then this is your counter program to the news," illustrates the exact irreverence that is a hallmark of the Jester archetype. It is not just play, but individual expression surrounded by a childlike point of view.

Stewart has also used humor and self-deprecation to get everyone to not only stop taking themselves so seriously, but so that he does not take himself so seriously. When he said "I can be in 20 movies, but I'll never be an actor," Stewart highlighted his own personality, but also at the same time allowed us all to look at ourselves and gave us permission to really understand who we are and what we are, and are not, best at.

It is this ability to be in the moment, to not really worry about others' opinion of them, and a desire to impart joy that are the hallmarks of the Jester archetype.

Behaviors: Finding joy in both the everyday as well as the big picture is core to the Jester. When things are getting too serious, or people are over-fretting about the future, or becoming depressed while reminiscing about the past, the Jester feels an intense desire to play. To craft the moment so that everyone can just be joyous and remember what it was like when we were children.

It is not just about a desire to play that drives the Jester. You'll find yourself drawn toward a desire to try everything and anything, even things that are taboo or forbidden. This youthful desire to taste the world is very appealing to everyone in the Jester's tribe. Opening up curiosity and the joy of creativity in others is the hallmark of the Jester.

If you have the desire to expand curiosity, bring out the giggles in others, and create a sense of joy in your tribe, then the Jester Stone archetype will deeply resonate with you.

Expression: The Jester realizes the present moment is the only thing that we truly experience and is driven to enhance this moment in time.

Language: "You only live once. Enjoy life"

Darkest Fear: Being trapped in boredom or feeling stifled

THE EVERYMAN

"We are all created equal"

Summary: Connecting to everyone and feeling the inclusion of equality is primary to alchemists who express themselves through the Everyman stone. While other archetypes may have an outward component, in that they directly express themselves by standing out in some way, the alchemist who expresses the Everyman is working to bring everyone, including themselves, into the tribe, into the fold, to be accepted for the basic trait of being human.

Being able to see everyone as just part of the human experience and to cut through class lines or hierarchies is a unique strength of the Everyman archetype. Understanding that living life with inclusion and togetherness, providing for loved ones, and being a productive member of society is exactly what creates the hero in all of us. The motto "all men and women are created equal" creates a unique perspective about how the Everyman is expressed.

Desire: Expressing with the Everyman archetype is a unique experience because one of the main desires of this archetype is to not stand out, which essentially somewhat mutes its expression to the outside world. Although this archetype has a goal to not stand out, that doesn't mean they are not looking to connect. In fact, connection to others in their community is core to the Everyman. The connection is not to network or build value in the usual sense of the word. The connection is to truly touch everyone with an understanding of what it means to be human.

The intensity of an authentic connection to others in their tribe is vital to these alchemists. In our achievement driven culture, alchemists with this stone can bring together communities because they are not looking towards outside achievement but rather looking to bridge all the members of their tribe into one cohesive whole. The desire for a common connection gives them the ability to see loneliness in all its forms and to have an intense desire to alleviate it.

Example: Everyone, being part of the human condition, can understand and communicate with the Everyman archetype. In Latin the phrase "Unus pro omnibus, ones pro uno," meaning "one for all, all for one." offers insight into how this Stone views the world. This archetype truly resounds with those individuals who see the world as a fabric of solid citizenship.

The actor Matt Damon embodies the Everyman in his everyday life as well as at times in his on-screen characters. Matt plays Jason Bourne in the movies that carry that name. In those movies, although the character is a highly trained special agent, he truly tries to live his life in a common way. The character is the opposite of the flash and style of James Bond. Even though he has star power in Hollywood, Matt Damon maintains his everyman persona in his personal life. His quote

> "I'm not Brad Pitt or George Clooney. Those guys walk
> into a room and the room changes. I think there's
> something more … not average, but everyman about me."
> —Matt Damon

Matt has the ability to recognize in himself that his strength is in connecting with everyone, not just those who are the elite of Hollywood. That sense of representing all members of his tribe and not just a select few is powerful. It is what allows him to not just excel at his craft, but also enable others to feel the empathy he has for everyone in the tribe. That is the power of the Everyman archetype and the power of the alchemist who expresses through this stone. If you have a deep understanding of how everyone is working through being human, then you will resonate with the Everyman.

Behaviors: As the Everyman's tribe becomes more cohesive and settled, enjoying the sense of calm and certainty of acceptance into the group is a core behavior. It is not necessarily a desire to keep everything the same, but you'll notice you will gravitate towards doing things that maintain social cohesion above all.

Additionally, you'll find yourself as being very self-deprecating and working towards aligning how you express your persona so that it fits tightly with the common objectives of your tribe. Working for the common good as well as shying away from accolades and possibly being rattled by others who are in search of recognition is a hallmark of this archetype.

It is not about being the same as everyone else, as the archetype name implies. Rather it is about recognizing that everyone has a part to play when it comes to enhancing the common good. Recognizing every man, woman and child for our shared humanity will deeply resonate with the Everyman archetype.

Expression: Sharing a common understanding of everyone in the tribe.

Language: "All men and women are created equal"

Darkest Fear: Standing out for no special reason while excluding others.

THE CAREGIVER

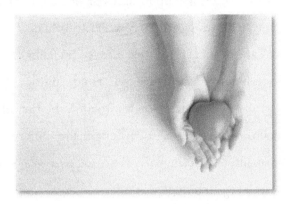

Summary: The Caregiver archetype is focused on compassion and generously taking care of others. Sometimes referred to as the Protector archetype, the Caregiver has an altruistic drive to help others. Expressing their PS through being nurturing and generous to others with their time and resources, especially others who are in need, is a driving force for this alchemist.

Many people who join the healthcare profession may express their Caregiver Philosopher's Stone in doing so. However, being in healthcare is not a requirement of the Caregiver PS. You can think of the attorney who helps with individuals in need, or an HR professional, or religious leaders all the way to Mother Teresa as examples of this archetype. If you think about changing the world, from yourself to your loved ones to your tribe to all those around you, then the Caregiver Archetype will resonate with you.

The Caretaker could be described as the Mother as well. It is not just about offering help in times of need. Caretakers take a nurturing, warm, thoughtful approach to others. They make others feel safe even in the most nerve-wracking times. It is offering preventative strategies to avoid injuries (whether physical, emotional, financial, or spiritual) in the first place. We all have a little Caretaker in our personality, but if thinking about the smallest suffering of others keeps you up at night, then the Caretaker archetype will ring true to you.

The motto of a Caregiver is "love your neighbor as yourself." That is a very clear message about how an alchemist with a Caregiver archetype, a Caregiver Philosopher's Stone, will interact with the outside world. They will always treat others in their tribe, and even others outside of their sphere of influence, with the same or better level of care and consideration as they would desire for themselves. This powerful message resonates with others. Caregivers become a safety net for their community since their primary focus is to nurture the entire group.

Desire: Being able to care for those in need or those who are in a vulnerable group is vital to this alchemical stone. Part of the way in which this stone is activated is by finding those within the community who will be better off with care, attention and nurturing. Providing the guidance and an environment that allows others to flourish creates a sense of accomplishment and is a hallmark of executing with this Philosopher's Stone.

You'll be fulfilled when you witness others grow, develop, and create the capacity to be completely self-sufficient. Recognizing that you have the resources within you to provide for others is key. It does not mean that you have exactly the form of resource that is wanted by others, but that within you, internal to your character, is the key you can use to take care of others. This is a significant distinction. You don't have to have everything for everyone, you individually will find and secure what is necessary for others to grow.

Additionally, alchemists with the Caretaker Stone will create environments that provide a feeling of safety and a place of belonging. Essentially, handcrafting the elements of being at home. The elements not just of comfort and the ability to relax and let your guard down, since the element of safety from outside forces has been handled, but also the elements that create an environment conducive to developing in all aspects.

The drive to not only help others, but to create a place of calm is key to this Stone archetype.

Example: Traditional examples of the Caretaker archetype are those in healthcare or directly in service. You can think of Mother Teresa as a perfect example of someone who expressed herself through a Caretaking Philosopher's Stone. However, it is not a requirement that you be in healthcare. A key example of a strong Caretaker alchemist is Ghandi.

Ghandi was a strong leader who brought independence to his countrymen. The leader component of Ghandi's personality is what allowed him to move large swaths of people to follow his lead. His deep desire to free his fellow citizens, to support their sovereignty without the need to resort to violence, is a clear example of his foundational drive to ensure his countrymen and women were taken care of from a civil point of view. It wasn't about taking care of their physical wellbeing, it was about taking care of their human drive to self-govern. As a trained lawyer, Ghandi did not have to spend the amount of time and energy he did to secure independence for his tribe, but his Caretaker archetype drove his life's work.

Two of Ghandi's quotes:

"The best way to find yourself is to lose yourself in the service of others"

and

"Service which is rendered without joy helps neither the servant nor the served."

—Ghandi

reflect his view of the world, that it is not just about himself, but is about the community (whether that community is just his local group of friends and family or if that community is the entire country). Ghandi, and all alchemists who express the Caretaker Philosopher's Stone, exhibit this community concern.

Behaviors: Caretakers scan the horizon looking for individuals or groups that would benefit from not just some TLC, but from real foundational support. That is the key. Alchemists who express their Philosopher's Stone through the Caretaker archetype are looking to create support systems that allow people to grow and flourish.

It is about creating the right soil that seedlings can plant themselves in and develop. The Caretaker can be seen looking to create safe spaces in all dimensions, from the physical to the emotional, from the tactical to the big picture. The Caretaker Stone is used to ensure that the outside environment supports the community's inside desires.

Think of Princess Diana and her fight against the use of landmines. Diana was the lead at the HALO Trust, which is an organization that removes landmines left over from war. Princess Diana not only focused on her local community (through her work with the Royal Marsden Trust which assisted with cancer treatment in London), but then found a worldwide issue she could address. Her work has been described as being influential in the signing of treaties to ban landmines.

Looking not just close to home, the Caretaker archetype will focus on the greater good of all communities to find a cause that can be advanced with care and attention. The desire to not just help those in need, but to also build safe spaces, will deeply resonate with those who have this Stone archetype.

Expression: Help those in need as well as build spaces that others can see as a safe haven.

Language: "Love your neighbor as yourself"

Darkest Fear: Finding ingratitude in themselves and others.

THE RULER

"Being powerful is like being a lady. If you have to tell
people you are, you aren't."
— Margaret Thatcher

Summary: The expression of an alchemist through a Ruler stone is not all about power, although it may seem that way from outside. Expressing your Prima Materia through the Ruler archetype is all about controlling chaos with the most direct method: By literally controlling or ruling over the chaos. The alchemist who authentically presents power through the Ruler Stone is the one who looks to be the Ruler so they can enhance the life of everyone in the kingdom. Moving from a Ruler into a mature and wise monarch or patriarch is the preferred path for all alchemists with this Stone.

Alchemists who express themselves through a Ruler archetype not only focus on controlling chaos, but actively embark on a journey to enhance the kingdom. This happens as the Ruler archetype evolves into a Monarch elevating the entire tribe from where they are to where they could be. This is a pure form of a Ruler, one who merges the enthusiasm of youth and the wisdom of the elders and then uses this union to elevate everyone in the kingdom.

Desire: The Ruler at a basic level is working to stem the chaos that can exist within a kingdom, whether they rule over that kingdom or not. The pressure of chaos that is created simply from being alive and living with a tribe within a kingdom is intense, and a benevolent Ruler is always trying to find ways to reduce this chaos. You will have an intense desire to create a calm environment (e.g., stemming the chaos of the tribe) by imposing order and rules.

You will also have a desire to create a way that provides for all members of your tribe, of your kingdom, a pathway to becoming better, not just for themselves, but for everyone. It is this desire to implement ideas that bring out the best of society as a whole that drives you. You will want to balance the natural entropy of growth with the calmness of a kingdom at peace. This constant balance between growth and calmness will be a core tension of how you engage with your Stone.

Example: It can be easy to mislabel alchemists who express themselves through the Ruler archetype both in that they can be miscategorized into other archetypes or all individuals who have certain jobs (e.g. politicians) can be lumped into the Ruler category. However, if you think deeply about the Ruler archetype, you'll notice they try and control chaos and elevate everyone in the kingdom through their position. Think of someone like Winston Churchill as a key example of an alchemist expressing himself through this archetype.

One of Churchill's quotes perfectly summarizes the Ruler archetype: "It is more agreeable to have the power to give than to receive." Even in the act of giving, which is to elevate others, the use of power to achieve end goals was the primary method. As Prime Minister of the United Kingdom twice, Churchill was concerned with creating a world that could not only withstand the chaos of World War II, but could also create a stable, enhanced life for his fellow countrymen. Although Churchill's policies and view are not without controversy and criticism, he has nevertheless been praised as a leader who created a stable society through some of the most turbulent times in history.

Behaviors: When an alchemist is pursuing calm in the midst of the storm, one of the best strategies is to prepare for the storm before it arrives. Churchill's quote, "it is always wise to look ahead, but difficult to look further than you can see," embodies this notion of vision. As a Ruler, looking into the future, especially when it is difficult to see just a bit further than the present, is key.

The behaviors of using rules and structure to create a calm environment as well as using rules and structure to enhance the tribe as a whole is something that will truly resonate with you as a Ruler alchemist. However, you will also start to try and understand what is around the blind corners of the future. Feeling uneasy with blind corners, which all alchemists do, is a natural reaction. The Ruler will attempt to create formalized systems in place to standardize the response to blind corners. You will notice this in your behaviors, that you feel most comfortable when you control the architecture of your tribe's responses to the external world.

A desire to create a harmonious world not just for those in your immediate circle, but for all of those from here to the horizon, will deeply resonate with alchemists projecting the Ruler Stone archetype.

Expression: The Ruler craves creating a prosperous community

Language: "Power isn't everything, it's the only thing"

Darkest Fear: Devolving into chaos, either personally or your tribe

THE CREATOR

Summary: Creators are driven by the desire to ... well ... create. To bring something into being that has not existed before. By completely surrendering to the process of creation as well as the final product, the creator connects with society and the universe by imprinting the world with an artifact of their self-expression. If you feel a driving desire to bring something into existence, no matter how big or small, no matter if it is a performance that only exists for an evening or something as grand as the Sphinx that lasts for millennia, then you will align with the Creator Stone archetype.

Desire: The creator views the act of creation as well as the object of art they create as a vehicle for their self-expression. Being authentic in what they create and how they create is fundamental to the Creator's journey. The creative journey itself is core to a Creator's expression. It is not just the final product that matters to the Creator, rather it is the path they took to produce the final product that has just as much, if not more, potency.

When a Creator is able to birth something truly unique, they are, for the moment, gaining control over an ever more uncontrollable existence. The creative process may be inherently unruly, but the Creator has complete control of each decision that is made through that process, and gains, for the moment, the ability to direct the outcome of a process that seems random, but is truly under the Creator's control.

Example: Steven Spielberg definitely embraces the Creator archetype. Just think about the broad spectrum of movies he has created: Jaws, Close Encounters, Raiders of the Lost Ark, ET, The Color Purple, Empire of the Sun, Schindler's List, Jurassic Park, and Saving Private Ryan. The breadth of his work is a roller coaster ride from suspense to action to adventure to drama. Each and every category a work of art in creation. Whether or not you appreciate his cinematic taste, Spielberg has re-written many of the genre's most loved stereotypes with his ability to craft a narrative given almost any set of circumstances. Just think about the narrative of Jaws. It's not about the shark, even though the shark is one of the main characters. Or think about the opening sequence of Saving Private Ryan, which completely transformed the traditional war movie.

Spielberg's ability to tap into our shared humanity is the paintbrush he uses to create imagery within a storied structure. He might have to constrain the story of Schindler's List within the context of a war movie, but his creative spirit required him to look deeper than the bullets and bombs and create; create something we could all connect to as humans. This is the drive of the Creator. The insatiable need to handcraft something unique and different no matter what the container.

Just think about his language:

"Every time I go to a movie, it's magic, no matter what the movie's about."

That's the language of creation. The creation of a magical moment.

"The public has an appetite for anything about imagination - anything that is as far away from reality as is creatively possible."

His goal is to feed the public's appetite for creation that stems from the recesses of our imagination.

Behaviors: Driven by a desire to create, sometimes the Creator is disagreeable or non-conformist. Conforming or being and behaving like everyone else does not allow for the pure spirit of creation. In fact, the ability to excel in a structured environment is defined not by creating something new, but rather by executing on what already is, which is antithetical to the Creator. Open, creative physical spaces allow creativity to flourish. Offices with open floorplans and workspaces without walls give space to creativity and Creators gravitate towards such environments.

Creating something unique, something that hasn't existed before, is extremely attractive to this archetype, since once you birth a creation that individually stands on its own, the Creator has inspired more than just their curiosity, they have expanded beyond themselves. In this way, the Creator archetype will work towards developing unique products. Don't think about just expanding features, but rather creating something completely new and different.

If you have this drive to birth the unexperienced, then the Creator Stone archetype will deeply resonate with you.

Expression: The creator expresses with the creative process. It is not necessarily the end product that is the goal, but rather the expression through the process itself.

Language: "If you can dream it, it can be."

Darkest Fear: "To be boring, stagnant, and stifled."

THE INNOCENT

Summary: Seeing the world and expressing your inner self through wonder, spontaneity and joy are all hallmarks of individuals who connect deeply with the Innocent archetype. Alchemists who express themselves through the Innocent will look for the simple truths in life that lead to great joy and the ability to see the potential for sacred beauty in all things.

Being able to always see the potential for joy in the world allows alchemists with this stone the ability to consider circumstances from an optimistic point of view. To always look for a way to experience life with optimism is truly unique to this archetype. An Innocent archetype will look for solutions to problems that have the least moving parts, meaning they are the simplest solution for achieving serenity. It is this ability to see the world in its purest form that is truly lovely about this individual.

Desire: When an alchemist expresses themselves through the Innocent Stone, they are really looking to engage with the core goodness in humanity as seen from a youthful perspective. The Innocent will have a drive to express humanity through simplicity and avoid the chaos that can be a hallmark of the complexities of the world.

Looking for the paradise of simplicity is part of being in a natural collective where each member of the tribe is part of the paradise. The Innocent archetype shies away from the angst that comes from competition. A pure desire to be cooperative with not only the members of their tribe but their environment itself is a core desire to this Stone archetype.

Example: Although Walt Disney may be perceived as a businessman or Imagineer, as he called the artists and engineers that helped him realize his dreams, he truly was an alchemist who expressed himself through a dreamer and Innocent archetype. Walt's desire to bring joy and happiness to the world, and especially the children of the world, was evident in all of his projects. From the animation, through to the creation of Disneyland, Walt's drive was to take the complexities of the world and simplify them into a magic moment of joy.

That is what makes Walt Disney such an iconic figure. His ability to dream and take on the complexities of the world in pursuit of handcrafting a simple time. When designing

Disneyland, Walt blueprinted a main street that reminded him of his boyhood hometown and then expanded his vision from there to build a safe, wondrous world for children and adults to explore.

Even Walt's language shows his ability to dream innocent dreams.

> "That's the real trouble with the world.
> Too many people grow up."
> "Our greatest natural resource is the minds of our children."

> "Laughter is timeless, imagination has no age, dreams are forever."
> —Walt Disney

Just those quotes alone give a glimpse into how Walt expressed himself in the world. The idea that simple joy is not only achievable, but that we can all achieve it and it can be handcrafted is a core belief of Walt Disney. Infusing his company with this culture is what allowed Disney to grow and become the iconic organization it is today. Just remember Walt's quote:

"If you can dream, you can do it. Always remember that
this whole thing was started by a mouse."

—Walt Disney

Behaviors: Looking for the simple solution is a hallmark of the Innocent archetype. Sometimes that will mean having a visceral understanding of how the world works in all its complexities and then distilling those complexities down into a simple vision. That's your superpower. Your ability to see the world through both a glass-half-full optimism and a search for the simple truth that inspires.

Making sure your tribe is happy and free from worry will be a significant driver in your behaviors. This will include a drive to eliminate the unnecessary elements of the world and focus on a simpler and more honest expression. Think about the impulse you feel when the complexities of the world are overwhelming. The impulse to trim back sophistication to reveal the core of something. You might express that impulse by working on finding the simplest answer to the question, and the answer that provides the most joy to the people in your tribe or the people that your tribe touches.

Innocent archetypes express themselves by extracting out complexity, revealing truth, and rating themselves on how joyous others are. If you have this desire to bring the joy of youth to your tribe, then the Innocent Stone archetype will deeply resonate with you.

Expression: The Innocent creates a world of simple harmony.

Language: "We are all young and free"

Darkest Fear: Being constrained or abandoned and left alone.

THE SAGE

Summary: The pursuit of knowledge as a proxy for the pursuit of truth is what the Sage archetype is all about. Sorting out truth from illusion by using intelligence and accumulating knowledge and experience to build a foundation is key to this archetype. Taking the knowledge you have gained and disseminating this knowledge to others in your tribe will be of extreme interest if you carry the Sage archetype.

As you express your Sage PS you will look at the world with a skeptical eye and diligently pursue critical thinking in service to becoming an expert in a given area or situation. Although we may think of this alchemist as the teacher or expert or master, you may express your knowledge or expertise in a unique fashion. Maybe that fashion is through humor or an intense understanding of public policy. You may be teaching and guiding without having an explicit role.

Desire: The Sage is constantly searching for more knowledge and wisdom, in all ways, intellectual or through experience. Having an experience and learning new insights in a hands-on fashion are very attractive to this alchemist. It is the learning, in whatever form that learning takes, that will drive your behaviors. This is interesting, because behaviors that may appear grounded in the Explorer archetype will truly just be an expression of the Sage in the pursuit of truth through experience. Once you feel that you understand the truth in some field you will be drawn to offer that wisdom to your tribe.

That is the second component of this PS. The first is gathering knowledge in search of truth, and the second is disseminating that truth through spreading wisdom. It is the wisdom that comes from taking information and knowledge and turning that knowledge into actionable insights that is truly unique to this PS

Example: There are many examples of the Sage in both real life and popular culture. Just thinking about the cultural elders, oracles and teachers through history evokes a list of Sages such as Socrates, Confucius, the Buddha, and Einstein. But a deeper look lets you realize that individuals such as George Carlin, Chris Cuomo or Rachael Maddow also express the Sage archetype as they excavate the landscape in search of truth to pass on as wisdom.

Of course, the set of wise Sages would not be complete if we didn't include Yoda from Star Wars. Part warrior, part Oracle, part sorcerer, Yoda is a conglomeration of the knowledge seeking, wisdom expressing personalities that encompass all alchemists with the Sage PS. Even his simplistic quotes from Star Wars, such as: "Do or do not. There is no try," are designed to enlighten his pupil and disseminate wisdom in a most compact form.

Behaviors: Using knowledge as a way to control the chaos of living is something that you'll have to grapple with. There are times when the search for understanding is colored by a desire to control the uncontrollable and consequently the search itself becomes uncontrollable. That is where you will have to be careful to understand why you are searching. If you are searching for enlightenment, the search will be fruitful. However, if you are searching just to keep the darkness at bay, then you will quickly find the search similar to running down rabbit holes that have no end.

There are two components to knowledge that are interesting to the Sage. The intellectual and the experiential. Combining both of those paths will provide a very rewarding experience and be a thrilling part of the growth of your Sage personality. Explore the experiences that will provide insight, don't just understand them, live them, fully engage with them.

Once you understand that head/heart, body/mind, intellect/spirit are all places you can find wisdom, you'll be drawn to all the facets of your personality.

Expression: The Sage searches for knowledge in the pursuit of truth and searches for truth in the pursuit of wisdom to share.

Language: "The truth will set you free"

Darkest Fear: Falling victim to falsehoods disguised as truth

THE EXPLORER

"You belong somewhere you feel free"

—Tom Petty

Summary: The Explorer archetype wants to break free. To shatter the shackles that bind them to where they are, so they can explore and find their true authentic self. The exploration is both external as well as internal as the Explorer is always looking for new experiences to create true autonomy. There is a deep desire to expand horizons and push boundaries in pursuit of freedom. When you have an Explorer's Stone archetype your desire to hit the open road and gain an understanding of yourself through the open road will be strong.

The journey, the drive to see what's around the next bend, does not always need to be in the form of an external trip. As Marcel Proust said, "The real voyage of discovery consists not in seeking new lands but seeing with new eyes." This is the journey of self-discovery not through internal mediation but through interacting with the external world. Exploring other people, other places, and other situations is core to the Explorer, for their heart is in the exploration in order to come back home knowing themselves even better than before.

Desire: The Explorer looks for the road less traveled. This PS will drive you to do things that others have not done and go places that others have not visited. It is your desire for self-understanding through the reflection of the external world that is vital. Your stone will create a craving for new experiences. Doing the same activity over and over will feel confining. Even if the activity is the same type of activity, like a long bicycle ride each weekend, you will feel compelled to take different paths each time, to see new scenery each time, to know new terrain on each encounter.

Although you may not feel a need to be a loner, your PS will guide you towards new experiences and individualistic pursuits. Sometimes it may be hard for others to keep up with your ability to jump from daily routines and push to the edge. Exploring the edge and discovering the newest boundary is key to this Stone archetype.

Example: A great example of the Explorer archetype is the British adventurer Bear Grylls. Grylls is widely known for his television series Man vs. Wild, which as a title in itself is almost a perfect description of the Explorer. As a former SAS serviceman, then a survival instructor, then writer and businessman, Grylls' drive to explore the newest personal terrain is just as strong as his drive to explore the physical world. At 23, he summited Mount Everest and in 2005 set the world record for the highest open-air formal dinner party at 25,000 ft. It is this drive to explore who he is internally through the mirror of the outside world that is emblematic of Grylls' PS.

Bear's quote *"You only get one chance at life and you have to grab it boldly"* is a testament to the power of this PS in how he focuses his efforts and makes decisions. Bold, expansive behavior that is beyond the bounds of traditional restraints is all part of how this PS is expressed.

Behaviors: Using the outside world as a mirror to discover the most authentic version of your internal self is essential to the Explorer. Always pushing boundaries in order to better understand yourself, where the edges of you stop and the outside world begins, gives the Explorer a map of their internal territory in relation to the outside world. You will feel a desire to push boundaries and discover new territories. This might show up in a drive to physically explore new territories in your professional life or to open new markets.

Being able to build a map of the previously unexplored is very seductive to the Explorer and their PS is fully activated when they get a chance to see the new and come back with an understanding of what is out there. Think about how tempting it is to map out what currently is unknown, and you'll have an idea of what this Stone archetype is best suited for. Opening new markets, using new tools, and mapping out new territories fall in the sweet spot of the Explorer Stone archetype.

Expression: The Explorer ventures into the unknown and maps out a world previously hidden.

Language: "Let me roam free"

Darkest Fear: "Being trapped and required to conform"

OPERATIONAL LENS

We've seen that your internal character is how you consume the world; it is your Prima Materia. We've seen that your archetype, the way you express, is your Philosopher's Stone. The last piece is your actual craft, whether that is your job, your career, or what you do with as much of your time as you can.

Think of your Operational Lens (OL) as the way you express your personality in the outer world, which is what we'll call your craft. That craft might be as a musician, a writer, an engineer, an entrepreneur, a teacher, or in law enforcement. The craft that you have chosen is what your OL looks like to the outer world. Your craft is how you express your inner PS, your inner dialogue.

For example, musicians express themselves to the world through sound. Through melody, or beats, a groove, or orchestrations. They see the world through notes: Half notes, whole notes, rests, scales.

A sound engineer also experiences the world through sound, but in a completely different way. A sound engineer thinks of discrete sounds. They think of a lion's roar, or the hiss of a steam pipe. A sound engineer thinks of tone quality or the attack and decay of a sound.

The musician and the sound engineer each have their own different OL. They express their craft in completely unique ways.

Your job, career or craft is the expression of your PS in the real world. It is the way you interact with the outside world. If your craft is as a baker, you'll interact with the world through food. If your craft is as a musician, you'll interact with the world through music. If your craft is entrepreneurship, you'll interact with the world through business and startups.

Each person's Lens is different and unique to them. Although all musicians see the world through notes and music, they don't all interact with the world through the same set of glasses.

Your Philosopher's Stone is the unique way you see and engage with the outside world. A jazz musician will see the world through scales and intervals. A C-Mixolydian scale here, a flat 13th interval there, an improvisation to be handcrafted over chord changes. That is the how the world reflects off the hand polished jazz musician's Stone.

A rock and roll musician will interact with the world very differently. A rock and roll musician might experience music as chord changes and lyrical phrases. That is how the world will reflect off their hand polished rock and roll musician Stone.

However your unique personal craft is expressed, make no mistake, it is there, and it does reflect the light of the outside world in a very particular way. Knowing and embracing your lens, your craft, is vital in your alchemical journey.

It took me a long time to find and embrace my own personal Operational Lens. Not only could I not see my lens when I was a young man, I was in fact attempting to dig up and polish blurry pieces of glass.

Glass that had been buried deep in the soil of society, and I certainly had no idea how to create a lens out of any of the pieces of glass I was finding.

You see, I love ideas. I love new ideas, tuning existing ideas, sharpening the effectiveness of newly born ideas. I love innovation and the choices that go along with innovating new concepts. Strategic direction operating within an unknown environment all wrapped in a social context, business or otherwise. But when I was young, I could not think in this fashion; I didn't know how. Until that fateful day at UCLA.

I didn't understand that my OL is most keenly focused when I am in full pursuit of understanding ideas.

That first class at UCLA when the professor told me that "Economics is not the study of money. It is the study of choice. Choices that you don't even think you have a hand in, but you do," adjusted my OL so that I could finally see clearly.

When I heard that language I understood, in my gut, what the professor was saying and why he was saying it. I had an "ah ha" moment when everything became clear. I was finally discussing big ideas. My Prima Materia and Philosopher's Stone were aligned and focused through my Operational Lens. For me that was Economics and Entrepreneurship.

This is what you are looking for. You are looking for the alignment of your Prima Materia and Philosopher's Stone to be magnified through your Operational Lens, through your craft, through what pulls you from your slumber when you are asleep.

BRINGING IT ALL TOGETHER

We've done a deep dive into how to Know Thyself. We've discussed:

Prima Materia: The core matter from which you are made. Usually you can't see it, but it becomes expressed in your personality and in how you consume information and situations in the world.

Philosopher's Stone: How you express yourself to the world. This is taking the Silly Putty of your Prima Materia and handcrafting the way you use it to interact.

Operational Lens: Applying your Prima Materia and Philosopher's Stone in what you do every day and what you bring to the world, typically in a professional setting, is what your operational lens is all about.

Prima Materia = How you understand the world

Philosopher's Stone = How you express yourself

Operational Lens = The physicalizing of your talents in the world.

Knowing thyself is about aligning all three elements.

In my case, I didn't really know how to do this until I was well into my adult career. I started going to college to become a doctor, an MD. My Prima Materia is all about exploring big picture concepts and coming up with my own ideas about how things operate. That's how I consume the world. I am constantly looking for big concepts, instead of getting really good at the details of one area. And once I understand the big picture, I tend to come up with my own way of doing things (this is expressed as having a high score on Openness and a low score on Agreeableness in the Big Five Personality model). As you can guess, this might be a good personality for an entrepreneur, but not necessarily the right Prima Materia for the world class surgeon that I wanted to become. Ok, so Prima Materia to MD ... not a great fit.

Then there's my Philosopher's Stone as evidenced by really finding that I completely align with the Magician. Guess what? The magician is all about digging into a subject, finding the basic building blocks and then re-assembling them into a new way of doing things. Nope, that does not fit with the kind of career I was looking for in medicine. So, Philosopher's Stone to MD ... not a great fit.

Alright, so trying to go to college and enter the medical profession didn't align my Prima Materia and my Philosopher's

Stone with the Operational Lens of being a doctor. That is the definition of being out of alignment.

It took me a while to realize that my Prima Materia consisting of being hungry for the big picture, plus my Philosopher's Stone of being hungry to understand the core components of ideas, were perfect for operating as an entrepreneur. Once I understood that this alignment is vital, I was finally able to embrace my Alchemical Persona and move my professional focus to entrepreneurship.

This is what you should be aiming for as well: Alignment. Aligning your Prima Materia and Philosopher's Stone with your Operational Lens. That will allow you to fall in love with your life, your career, your passion, and really start turning lead into gold.

5. THE ALCHEMICAL TRANSFORMATION

Turning lead into gold. That's what we're really after, metaphorically speaking. The modern-day version of taking base metals like lead or mercury and, after some magical process, turning those metals into precious metals like gold or silver. That's what we think of as the alchemists of lore. Crazy-haired wizards searching wildly for some way to magically create something valuable out of common materials. Or maybe you think of a mad scientist searching for the secrets of immortality on a valiant yet always futile quest. Maybe that is what you have been exposed to when it comes alchemists and their goals. Actually, alchemists can probably be credited with many ideas that have informed modern day chemistry and experimentation, like the process of distillation. You can think of Isaac Newton or Tycho Brahe as well-known alchemists who were searching to distill some of the most basic ideas into cohesive theories, which is, in itself, a type of alchemy.

But when and how does the transformation take place? That is where we are now. The Alchemical Transformation itself. The steps we can take to turn something common into something of great value.

Although the caricature of the transformation is to create manmade gold, the real value does not lie in the end product itself (the gold); the real value lies in understanding how the transformation works. Because once you understand the process of transformation, you can start to transform all sorts of things.

That's the most important part. It is not about turning one piece of lead into gold, it is about

LEARNING THE PROCESS OF TRANSFORMATION

Once you know to transform something, you can do it over and over again.

Throughout history, the alchemical process of transformation has taken many different forms. There are all sorts of recipes. Some with 7 or 12 steps, some have 20 stages, and there are 50+ step versions as well. As students of innovation, Synaptic Alchemists look to find a version of the alchemical process that is easy to understand and use on a day-to-day basis. Too many steps and being overwhelmed with too much information can be just as stifling as not having enough, which is why we are going to distill the alchemical transformation down to its most basic components.

In the West, there have been many explanations of the alchemical process and historically they all have a consistent four-part process. For our purposes, we will simplify that even further down to a three-step process. That makes it even easier to understand and use day-to-day.

That's it. Just three simple steps to learn how to turn lead into gold, ideas into businesses, thoughts into new products and services and mindsets into public policy. Three stages keep things simple. However, remember, simple does not mean easy. It is not easy to see how these three steps will eventually play out in advance. That is the simple but not easy part. Just because you might not be able to clearly see an obvious way to apply these steps doesn't mean there isn't a path that you can walk with success today. All successful ideas and business have used these steps, whether they knew it at the time or not.

Read that again.

ALL successful ideas and business HAVE GONE THROUGH the three-step model of Synaptic Alchemy.

Remember Synaptic Alchemy is all about taking an idea from your head and imprinting it in the real world so that it turns into something valuable, some type of gold. This is about innovation, not about magic. It is about understanding what the path looks like when you turn something as ephemeral as an idea into something that is truly valuable. That can be a new entrepreneurial business, a public policy, a new product in a large company, or a new career.

The Synaptic Alchemical Transformation has three big sections:

1.) Destroy Something

2.) Create Something

3.) Standardize Something

We'll discuss the details behind each of these sections as well as look into how they apply to you in particular and explore examples of those who have already gone through the process. With that in mind, let's get started.

The Three Steps of Alchemy

We are about to take a deep dive into the steps and paths of the Synaptic Alchemist and the Alchemical Transformation. There is all sorts of stuff to cover here, from big ideas to tactical activities. It can be overwhelming. No one does this all at once. The Alchemical Transformation is a mindset, a thought process that, once discovered, you will carry with you always. You'll start to see the world through this lens. Do not worry if you are not doing every single step for every single idea you have immediately. Once you get these ideas under your fingers, you'll apply them when they are needed. However, if you have the temperament, you could start the alchemical process for your current passion, see how far you get, and see where it will lead you. I believe that you are highly likely to be led to a path that you didn't expect.

We know there are three steps to the Synaptic Alchemy process: Destroy something, Create Something, Standardize

Something. But what does that really mean? Let's go through a high-level exploration of each step.

Destroy Something: Called Nigredo in traditional Alchemy. Destroying something sounds really harsh. It sounds, well, destructive. Do you really have to blow something up to turn lead into gold? Well, not in the physical sense. No, you don't need to go out and destroy your competition or tear your office apart. You do, however, need to look at how things are happening in the real world and decide that they don't need to be done that way anymore. The term "creative destruction" was coined by economist Joseph Schumpeter back in the 1940's. He discussed this as an economic idea where new products replace old ones. The theory of creative destruction is much more complex than just that sound bite, and it affects the economic landscape at both the macro and micro level. In SA terms, we talk about destroying something in the context of the disruption economy by looking at the IDEA of how things are currently done and deciding that it doesn't need to be that way any longer.

It is easy to see this in action with hindsight. Think about Amazon.com. Remember when Amazon first started? They started with the idea and goal of being the world's largest bookstore. The idea that a bookstore had to be a physical building holding a certain number of books is what Amazon's founder and current CEO Jeff Bezos destroyed. Books, and eventually everything else, didn't need to be held in a retail building. That idea was revolutionary at the time: No Buildings to Buy Books. He destroyed the idea that books needed to be sold in-person.

Create Something: Called Albedo in traditional Alchemy. Once you have destroyed something, once you have decided that an old idea is worth getting rid of, you have to replace it with something new. The need, the thing that the old idea was serving, is still around, but once the old way of doing things is obsolete, something new must fill the void. That "create something" mindset is what will discover a way to fill that need in a new and improved way. When something is deconstructed, i.e. destroyed in the Nigredo stage, we tend to think of that as negative. But it is just a change, and with that change comes opportunity, the opportunity to evolve to a new way of thinking and of doing. That's Albedo in a nutshell. It is the evolution opportunity.

Let's continue using Amazon.com as the example. If books don't belong in stores anymore, then where do they belong? Well, they don't belong anywhere in terms of a store. They belong in readers' hands, whether that is in digital or physical form. So, what did Amazon create? They created the idea that any book could be in your hands quickly (and in terms of the

Kindle instantly) WITHOUT visiting a store. The idea of books not being in bookstores would have been unthinkable without the converse idea of books direct to consumers. Think about that. When Amazon.com started they kicked off the DTC (direct to consumer) trajectory of books. Although publishers are still around in the distribution of books, Amazon's transformation of books removed one of the elements of the supply chain.

Standardize Something: Called Rubedo in traditional Alchemy. You've identified an idea that is old school and can change. The old rule. Then, you've identified a new school idea that can replace it. The new rule. Now turning the new rule into something so simple that it can be easily done and eventually becomes synonymous with the task itself is the goal of all alchemists. This is key to making any idea, product or service sticky: standardization. When the new idea of Albedo becomes so automatic that it becomes the new normal, you have truly turned lead into gold.

Amazon has become the standard not just for books but for commerce in general. Shopping online, and shopping with next day, and in some cases same day, delivery has become the new wave of shopping. From books to electronics to groceries, the idea that customers will walk into stores has been transformed into a new standard. That's the final step in

Synaptic Alchemy. It isn't that we don't shop for books anymore. It is that books are delivered to our door next day or to our devices instantly. Alchemy in its purest form.

NIGREDO

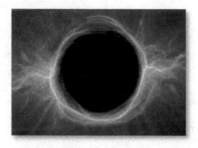

The blackness. It sounds as nerve wracking as it feels. Alchemists of the past believed that this was the first step in creating the Philosopher's Stone. However, for us modern Synaptic Alchemists, we have assumed that your Philosopher's Stone has already been created as part of Knowing Yourself.

So, Nigredo, the blackening, will be the first step in turning a specific idea from just an idea into something tangible. The blackness is all about dissolving an old idea. Dissolving an old way of doing things. Dissolving the old rules to make room for the new. The new part happens in the next step. But first we have to figure out what is going to get dissolved or transformed away.

Looking backwards in history it is easy to see what was dissolved. Hindsight is always 20/20 when it comes to innovation. However, seeing what happened successfully in the past is very different from being able to replicate it in the future.

Why Nigredo?

Why do we have a step where we need to think of something that needs to be destroyed? That's a great question. Glad you asked. Because it seems like a strange type of thinking, but it is the type of thinking that all good innovation and innovators go through. Let's think of what innovation really means. Thought leaders have described innovation in all sorts of ways:

- Ideas that add value from a customer's perspective

- Ideas that are novel and useful

- Ideas that are perceived as new by customers

- Ideas that bring constant value to the customer

You'll notice a common theme in these definitions. To provide something new that matters to the customer. It is the new part that is common. The new implies that the customer will do something different, think about something in some new way, or behave in a completely unique manner.

To do things differently, customers will have to drop something they are currently doing in order to do the new thing.

It is the "drop what you are currently doing or thinking" part that is the basis of Nigredo. If we all just kept doing things the same way we have in the past then innovation would come to a grinding halt. That's why Nigredo is important. The first step to innovation is to let go of the old to make way for the new.

But that's hard to do in real time. Because we think that everything we are doing today is necessary—it must be done.

Think about a fish. A good ole' fish is simply swimming around happily going about its day. The fish really has no idea about the water they are swimming in. Water is just part of the everyday environment. A fish can be swimming in a dirty pond or a crystal-clear lake, but swim around they will, all without noticing the water they are swimming in.

That is how we are. Happily going about our day in our environment not really noticing if the water we are swimming in could be ... well ... better. Not really noticing if we thought about our water, thought about different water, or no water at all, what type of innovations we could come up with. That's why the thought experiment represented by Nigredo is important.

The Nigredo Mindset

Synaptic Alchemy is all about creating something that didn't exist before. The Nigredo step is about figuring out what old rules no longer apply, which is hard to see ahead of time. It is kind of like creating a scrumptious new dessert that has never existed before, but without a recipe to follow. So, not only do you need to create the new dessert, you also have to figure out what ingredients to use, how to cook it, how to plate and serve the dessert and do all of this without any guidance.

It would be great to have a recipe—a set of steps—to help us walk down a path of innovation when it comes to blowing away an old idea. But there are no sets of standard steps for innovation. Instead of a recipe, you need a mindset. A new way of thinking. A new paradigm. To help us shape our new mindset, there are three steps you can use to focus your attention when you are in the blackness of Nigredo.

1.) The old What: Identify an old idea that either no longer serves its purpose or serves its purpose in an inefficient manner.

2.) The real Why: Tease out the actual purpose of the old idea.

3.) The Alternate Reality: Understand how customers would behave if the old idea didn't exist.

An understanding of how these mindset touchstones work can be illustrated through history. Let us take a look at how those three steps allowed Amazon to become one of the world's most valuable brands.

1.) The old What: Books have to be sold at bookstores. That's the old idea. Because, as we have all seen, books actually DON'T need to be sold in physical retail stores. A physical store is too small to fulfill the large selection needs of customers. When Amazon was first being born, they were the "World's Largest Bookstore," but had no stores.

2.) The real Why: A main component of bookstores was the assumption that customers want to start reading their books immediately, so they need access to physical copies at their fingertips. But actually, customers will wait for the specific book they are interested in reading. Even if that wait is only overnight (think Amazon Prime).

3.) The Alternate Reality: What would people do if bookstores suddenly evaporated? Would they stop reading? Nope, people would still read, they would just find other ways or places to get the texts: Libraries, sharing circles, or handwritten texts.

If you look at these three steps, it becomes clear that people will always read information or creative works, that they will wait a short period of time to get their product, and they need a larger selection than can typically be carried in a traditional physical store.

Those three aspects of Nigredo provided a substantial foundation to Amazon's idea to disintermediate the bookstore industry. You notice that at the beginning they were just looking to change how books were sold, not necessarily how books were published. They were in the business of disrupting how books were bought, not how they were created (they changed that later in their evolution).

THE OLD WHAT

What exactly does that phrase mean? "The old What"

It is identifying an idea, a way of doing things, or a belief, and questioning if that belief is still relevant, is performing a function that people still need, or is still as efficient as it could be in performing that function.

Exposing this line of thinking is similar in context to Professor Clayton Christensen's "Jobs to Be Done" framework[23] in that a direction of innovation should come from the jobs that customers are trying to accomplish. That is analogous to answering the following question:

"What is my customer doing?"

This is a harder question to answer than it appears at first glance. You have to really catalog the steps your customer takes when they are attempting to accomplish a goal before you really understand what the goal is. That's because people in general are operating in an automatic fashion. We don't typically think: 'I need to get THIS thing done because of THAT reason."

This quote by Harvard marketing professor Theodore Levitt perfectly expresses this situation.

"People don't want to buy a quarter-inch drill. They want a quarter-inch hole."[24]

—Theodore Levitt

In reality we are not even looking for quarter-inch holes. We are looking for the hole to do something. Maybe that something is to hang a picture or put up a shelf. And in reality, hanging the picture or putting up the shelf isn't really something we are looking for. Maybe we are looking to beautify our home or looking to create space in a cluttered garage. The end result, the final job-to-be-done in Christensen's terms, is what we are looking for.

Think about this in the context of doing a common task. Just imagine something simple like buying a birthday gift for someone you care about. You are going shopping for a gift. You are going to buy something. But you are not really shopping for any old thing. You are shopping for something that will bring a smile to their face. That's what you are really doing. You are shopping for a smile.

IDEO, the iconic design thinking firm, infuses their process with an exploration of what makes the customer tick. It is this drive to understand, to illuminate the jobs we do every single day in a given scenario, that imparts the mindset of Nigredo to the IDEO team.

I have personally experienced this mindset when I was with my last company. It took me a long time to figure out what my customers really wanted. On so many occasions I thought I knew what they wanted. But what I THOUGHT they wanted was usually just a target or symptom of what they were really looking for.

We executed a technical task at this company. A task that is very specific to a very narrow industry. We performed medical second opinions. That is what my customers bought and so I thought that is what my customers wanted. At least that is what they said, and believed, they wanted. They wanted a specialist physician to review the notes and facts of a medical decision and to give their point of view. But that big statement, "we want medical second opinions," was not the whole story.

How did we find that out? Because, at the beginning, we gave them high quality medical second opinions. And they went … Meh. They kind of shrugged their shoulders, were unimpressed, and many of our sales calls didn't convert into actual sales. That left me and my team in a serious quandary. What did our customers really want?

That is a really hard question to answer without knowing what everyone does on a daily basis. So, we started to watch them, and ask them two questions:

1.) How have you done this in the past?

2.) Do you really want to do that?

And you know what? They gave us good answers. One simple example was that they would fax original medical records to the doctors. Hundreds and hundreds of pages of test results, diagnosis, and analysis would be faxed from one doctor to another. That is how information was exchanged, via fax. That is the way they were doing things in the moment.

What is interesting is that our customers really didn't want to be faxing entire books of documents from one doctor to another. They saw that as a waste of time and fraught with errors. They didn't know if the doctor on the receiving side really received everything that was sent, and it was difficult to keep track of whether or not they had already sent something.

Spending many days shadowing and sitting right next to our clients in the field, watching what they did on a consistent basis and then asking them what they'd like not to do any more provided insights that drove our decisions. These decisions were completely different than what we had done in the past. In the past, we had focused on the steps in the medical second opinion, what we had now was a way to see what was causing our customers real concern.

That is the beauty of "The old What." It forces you to start to see the world through your customers' eyes, ears, and hands. You have to start seeing things through their eyes and walking in their shoes. That gives you unique insight into what they are doing and possibly, just possibly, an insight into what could be blackened.

Asking those two questions:

1.) How have you done this in the past?

2.) Do you really want to do that?

Become key to understanding the "old What"

What does the past look like?

Asking people to see far into the future can be hard When you watch what people actually do in recent situations, you get a chance to see their true behaviors and not just what they will tell you they did or think they did. It is those behaviors that will give you clues to things that can be blackened.

Don't just rely on verbal descriptions of what people have done in the past. In general; we tend to remember things differently than what actually happened. Our memories of the past are vulnerable to change. Daniel Schacter of Harvard University has stated[25] that

> "when someone first records a memory, the view incorporates his or her own reactions and inferences about the event. As a result, the viewer can color or distort the memory from the very beginning."
>
> —Daniel Schacter

That's just when a memory is recorded. We can distort memory when we try and recollect them as well.

> "When you recall a memory, it is not just simply read out, you have to store and consolidate [stabilize] it again."
>
> —Daniel Schacter

Consequently, memories can be colored and become vulnerable to both internal and external influences.

This is especially true for activities that we may not enjoy, that take longer than we wish, or we do by rote memorization. Our ability to recall or estimate past tasks is subject to many cognitive biases, including: optimism, overconfidence, framing, anchoring, mathematical ideal, and the planning fallacy. There are so many ways we can misremember our activities in the past that the best way to see how things have been done and how they are being done is to:

WATCH

Observing people in their natural habitats working or doing the tasks or chores that you are thinking might have some old rules embedded in them IS KEY.

Don't just ask: "How have you done this in the past?" Ask if you can shadow or watch and then record what people are doing. It's a type of anthropology, and key if you are going to go after an old rule or old way of doing things. It is crucial to Nigredo.

But what if you can't directly observe? Well, then you'll need to observe in some indirect way. Interviewing. Reviewing the artifacts that have been produced. Reviewing videos.

Anything to get as close to the way an old rule is being executed as possible.

THE TRADITION

Amazon gives us a chance to see Synaptic Alchemy in action in one of the most publicly visible ways possible.

A question for Amazon at the time Jeff Bezos was developing his concept of "The World's Largest Bookstore" was "Why Books?" A June 1997 video featuring Bezos[26] reveals an insight into his mindset when he stated:

> "in the book space there are over 3 million different books worldwide active in print at any given time across all languages, more than 1.5 million in English alone. So, when you have that many items you can literally build a store online that couldn't exist any other way."
>
> —Jeff Bezos, CEO Amazon

The last part of that quote is key, "you can literally build a store online that couldn't exist any other way." Think about that. That implies that books are searched for, hopefully found (kind of a needle in a haystack when a typical indie bookstore might hold 5,000 titles and even a big chain bookstore might hold 50,000 titles), or ordered so they can finally be put into the hands of the customer.

By answering the question "How has this been done in the past," Bezos instinctually discovered a way of doing things that was inefficient and didn't really give the customer what they wanted in a truly satisfying way. This is how Bezos discovered the old rule, the old way people were acting. By finding the old rule, Bezos was able to find something he could take away, the old rule, and eventually replace with a new way of thinking (that's the Albedo phase).

Back in 1997, the traditional way——how we did things in the past—of discovering and consuming the information in a book was to visit a bookstore. I'm sure you remember browsing the aisles of your local bookstore looking for something to read. In terms of discovering a new book, either you went through the aisles browsing or you got a recommendation. Maybe that recommendation was from a friend or maybe you heard an interview with the author. Then you went to the bookstore to purchase the book. Maybe they had it in stock, maybe they had to order it. That was the tradition, the old way of buying.

But we didn't want ink on paper. We weren't buying wood pulp with characters printed on them. We were buying knowledge or entertainment. That's the old rule that Amazon disintermediated. The words in the book, the thoughts in the book, the story in the book is what we were really looking for.

Google changed the world in a similar fashion. Yahoo! was launched in 1994 and already had its IPO in April 1996[27].

Yahoo! created a web directory, manually curating and categorizing websites into their directory. In 1998, Google founders Larry Page and Sergey Brin attracted the attention of Sun co-founder Andy Bechtolsheim, who wrote them a check for $100,000 and Google Inc. was officially born[28]. Page and Brin looked at the traditional way of categorizing the web (which was from Yahoo!, only a couple of years old, and all manual) and decided that the traditional way just wasn't going to work. Instead of human categorizers (who were originally known as "the surfers"), the Google team created an algorithm. Originally called "BackRub" because the system checked backlinks to estimate the importance of a site, Google's new algorithm called PageRank was automated. The old rule—use humans to categorize—was replaced with the new rule—use an algorithm.

This is a core example of tradition being an entry point for Nigredo. Even if tradition is only a couple of years old. In 1998 Yahoo! Had the chance to license the new search technology created by Google for $1 million, but they passed. Yahoo!'s core business was sold to Verizon in 2016 for $5 billion. Google's market cap as of today (September 2020) is just over $1 trillion.

The power of understanding a tradition that has outlived its time and is disintermediated through Nigredo has never been more apparent than in the Google-Yahoo! example.

WOULDN'T YOU RATHER?

Think about how you view the tasks you accomplish on a daily basis. What consistently comes to mind? The most enjoyable parts of your day-to-day activities or the parts that are uncomfortable? For most people, we are finely tuned instruments on what is not working, not feeling good, or is problematic. As a species we definitely know how to focus on the glass half-empty part of our daily routines.

There is a cognitive bias appropriately called the Negativity Bias. It simply states that, all other things being equal, we tend to feel and pay attention to negative circumstances more than we do positive ones.[29] While there is a substantial amount of psychological research on negativity bias, just understanding that people spend more energy processing negative tasks will provide you with unique insights.

By trying to answer the question: "Do you really want to do that?" You are implicitly looking for small places in a process or a customer's journey that are ripe for disruption or, in Synaptic Alchemy terms, are ready for Nigredo.

On average, people will be able to tell you what they don't want to do, rather than some vague idea of what they would rather be doing. The straightforward tactical understanding of having to do something, coupled with the aggravation of doing that thing, is quite easy to recall.

Think about the last time you were stuck in traffic. Or the last time you had to wait in a long line, or fill out a long form, or, or, or. I bet you can easily recall those moments. And if you were asked, "do you really want to be stuck in traffic?" the answer would definitely be a resounding "No." Your job as a Synaptic Alchemist is to really understand, at a core level, what your customers DON'T want to do.

Let us take the example from my last company of faxing volumes of medical information from one doctor to another. When we asked "do you really want to fax 100's of pages" the obvious answer was, of course, always no. The follow-up question of "what are you trying to do then?" is what led my team to understand the customer. "We need to get this important information to the doctor in its original form." That was a key insight. Faxing was the only tool my potential customers had at the time to get information from one expert to another "in its original form." The original form was important because this was medical information that could not have anything changed during transmission.

So, the "Do you really want to do that?" question coupled with "What are you trying to do then?" are the two keys to uncovering possible areas ripe for Nigredo type disruption.

THE REAL WHY

Now that we are getting an understanding of old rules, old "whats" that our audience is acting on, we can start to get down to the motivation behind the question. Asking "Why?" gets down to the heart of the matter. Once you know WHAT your customer does on a daily basis, it is vital to understand WHY they do it.

Many times, people do something for what they think is a clear-cut reason but, in the final analysis, what they do is usually only related to why they do it in a very roundabout way.

Understanding the core reason something is done is very powerful. Once you understand the why, you are in a position to change people's direction or point of view.

In digging for "The real Why", you are looking for what Chris Voss, former lead international kidnapping investigator for the FBI, and author of "Never Split the Difference:

Negotiating as if Your Life Depended on It,"[30] listens for. It is a simple two-word phrase:

"That's right."

When you hear that phrase, you are in alignment with WHY your customer or counterpart is doing the WHAT part. At that point you are starting to understand "The real Why" behind "The old What".

So how do you get there? What is the mindset to uncovering the real why?

When you ask someone why they do what they do, you are really trying to elicit their motive for taking the actions they take. Uncovering their motivation is vital.

The following two exercises will provide insights into motivations.

1.) The Repetitive Why Inquiry

There is an old business and sales mantra: "What are you selling?" If you ask this over and over again, taking the last answer and turning it into a question you'll start to dig down deep into people's motivation. I've heard this rephrased in many incarnations:

"What business are you in?"

"Why do you do that?"

It seems like a simplistic exercise. But it is revealing.

The technique has its roots in the repetition acting exercise developed by Sanford Meisner[31] where actors repeat each other's questions until they instinctually feel a motivation to change the question.

The Repetitive Why Inquiry is really easy to do. Ask "Why do you do that?" When the response comes back, add it to the end of the question and ask again. Here is a really simple example staying with our bookstore theme:

Q.) "Why did you go to the bookstore the last time?"

A.) "Because I wanted to get this specific book?"

Q.) "Why did you want to get that specific book?"

A.) "Because one of my colleagues recommended it"

Q.) "Why is it important that your colleague recommended it?"

A.) "Because this colleague is influential, and I will be seeing them at the next company meeting"

Q.) "Why is having the book by that meeting important?"

A.) "Because I want to have a deep conversation with them on the topic by then"

Statement: "So having read the book by the next company meeting will give you the background you need to have a deep conversation"

Answer: "That's right"

That is what you are looking for. That last statement. The understanding of the true motivation.

Realize that you will find many different motivations for the same action. In the book example, some people will want to finish books by a certain time, so they will be willing to wait to get the exact book in a couple of days, while others might need to read an article that summarizes the book immediately.

Being able to group people in your audience by motivations, by their Why, is a key differentiator for Synaptic Alchemists.

Motivation segmentation is very different from demographic and psychographic segmentation. In traditional audience segmentation, you are asking "who." As in, "who" is in a specific cohort? You've seen these descriptions many times, e.g. young men age 18-25 who read automobile articles. That gives you a picture of who these individuals are. However, understanding their why reveals a much deeper motivation, e.g. men who buy cars they can work on themselves in the privacy of their own garage to take them from average to perfectly running. The motivation segmentation is a very different cohort than the demographic and psychographic one.

A PERSONAL EXAMPLE

The Repetitive Why Inquiry might feel too easy or like it is not generating a unique insight at first. It certainly felt that way to me initially. But don't give in too quickly, because there is hidden value just under the surface.

I've had this happen to me so many times it is hard to count.

When running CID Management, I thought I understood my customer. We spent time watching the people on the ground, the employees who were responsible for working with doctors' decisions about patient care and getting second opinions when necessary. I thought I really understood why my customers did what they did.

I was wrong.

I knew I was wrong when I tried to predict the next action my customer would take but was consistently off.

I'll give you a really clear example. Faxing.

Yep, I know. Faxes are an old technology in this day and age of the 2020's. You would think that taking an analog input, like paper, turning it into a digital version via the fax, then printing that fax on the other side wouldn't be something that happens on a consistent basis. But it does. And I couldn't figure out why.

The team and I started asking questions. We started asking why our customers were faxing medical records and not sending them via email. We started asking why they were faxing the same document over and over again. We started asking why about everything.

We got answers. Sometimes answers that we didn't understand. But answers nonetheless. The answers became crystal clear in a couple of areas:

1.) We fax because that is what doctors use. They use faxes. Doctors are used to printed records, and since faxes are automatically printed out of the fax machine, they use faxes.

2.) Faxes go over phone lines. And real-time faxes are HIPAA compliant. Since doctors are considered a covered entity and have to worry about HIPAA compliance, they can fax medical records without having to worry about additional security safeguards.

Great. Two new answers as to why faxes are vital. We pivoted our communications focus from digital to faxes. Not that we got rid of our highly secure digital platform or digital communications R&D. But instead of going against the grain with regard to how our clients work, we went with the grain. We put in an effort to have our software use digital versions of fax machines. We automated the sending and resending of faxes, then put all that information into digital dashboards with fax buttons all over the place.

That gave us a differentiating factor in our business. Digital dashboards coupled with the ability to fax at the press of a button.

Faxes ended up being a unique piece of our lead to gold path that I would not have recognized if we didn't ask Why, over and over again.

2.) This Matters Because? (Judgment/value)

McKinsey & Company[32] is one of the most prestigious management consulting firms in the world. Founded in 1926 by James McKinsey, they now have over 100 offices internationally in 60 countries and count 60%+ of the Fortune 1000 as their clients. With revenue over $10 billion, they are one of the world's top collections of strategic minds. They are well known for asking "So What?" Former consultant Dr. Paul Friga discusses "Identify The 'So What(s)'" in his book "The McKinsey Engagement: A Power Toolkit for More Efficient and Effective Team Problem Solving".[33]

This question and line of thinking is where we as Synaptic Alchemists attempt to extrapolate the real motivations of our audience and the old rule and filter out false whys. Getting false positives in this arena can truly derail your search for true motivations. You will find that people in general will give you plenty of reasons why they do something, but those reasons are often not truly their motivations. Why do we do this? Our psychology drives a desire in us for two things:

1.) *Competency* - We want to be right. We want to be able to state that we clearly understand our reasons for our motivation and actions. Declaring that a specific action was motivated by a specific reason and then clearly violating that reason typically makes most people uncomfortable.

2.) *Certainty* - On average, most people have a hard time internally reconciling that they really don't know why they do what they do. Oh, you might meet someone who says "I don't know" quite a bit of the time. But if you continue to query them, they will quickly be able to tell you what they think is the reasoning behind their actions.

This is not to say that you won't find those who violate the above principles. They are guidelines. Yes, you will come across compulsive liars and psychopaths in your life. But, in general, people will want to show that they are correct and certain in why they do what they do.

Consequently, identifying the correct "So What" is vital to your alchemical exploration.

This is part of getting to the real Why. As an alchemist you can watch what people do, and then start to ask why they do it. In fact, the following experiment can be quite revealing:

1.) Observe what someone does (e.g. goes to a bookstore to buy a book)

2.) Ask them "Why did you do that?" This quite often will evince a blank stare as a response as it seems obvious. This is where the repetitive why exercise comes in.

3.) Wait for an answer, reverse the motivation and ask: "So, this is important because ..." Leave a pregnant pause. Of course, you'll want to word this in the way that seems best to you.

4.) Then ask, "What would happen if you didn't ..." Getting people to think about how the world would look if this thing didn't exist gives you a glimpse into what is really important to them.

Remember, people are programmed to think through the downside of things. Trust me. Put in the right question, word it in the right way, and you will definitely get an earful regarding why what they did is important.

That's where the gold lies. Right there. That is where the alchemical art form comes to us. Being able to take what they tell you about why it would be crazy to not do what they did and teasing out the golden nuggets.

"It's a Wonderful Life"[34] is the 1946 movie that is played each and every Christmas season, where the main character, George Bailey, decides it's all not worth it and is going to commit suicide on Christmas Eve. His guardian angel shows George the alternate reality of how different life would be for the people he cares about, his wife and community, if he had never existed.

There is a more modern movie from 1998 with Gwyneth Paltrow called "Sliding Doors"[35] that has a similar theme. The theme of the movie is that there are two storylines for Gwyneth's character's life. One storyline has one set of circumstances and the other is without those circumstances.

You can find these types of mental gymnastics in many other contexts from older parables to something as culturally mainstream as the 1999 movie the "Matrix[36]", where there are two realities, one gritty and physical and one pristine but generated by aliens. Neo, the main character, oscillates between each reality during the film.

That's the core tenet of "The Alternate Reality" exercise of Nigredo within Synaptic Alchemy. What we are looking for is what psychologists refer to as the "George Bailey effect."[37] This is where removing the presence of something and thinking about an alternate reality where that idea is absent can have a significant impact on behavior.

A 2008 study by Minkyung Koo & Sara Algoe, published in the Journey of Personality and Psychology,[38] discusses how contemplating the absence of something in our lives can have a real impact on how you perceive its value.

This is what we are looking for as alchemists. We are looking to take away the old rule, the old way of doing things; create an alternate reality in which what we do (the old what) is gone and force ourselves or our audience to think about how we would satisfy our need without the old what.

Think for a moment about Amazon. We have talked about this briefly before in the Nigredo Mindset. What would people do if bookstores suddenly evaporated? Would we stop reading? Would we stop sharing knowledge and entertainment. No, we would still read and share stories, it would just look different.

What would that alternate reality look like if bookstores were not the only place you could get books? That question in and of itself forces you to start to think about the intrinsic value of bookstores.

That's what we are looking for. A question. A process. A technique that allows us to tease out the intrinsic value of ideas. One that allows us to see clearly how we can take old rules, tease out their intrinsic values, keep those values, but re-cast the old rules into entirely new models.

ALBEDO

The whitening stage: A stage which is literally referred to as ablution, meaning the washing away of impurities. For the purposes of Synaptic Alchemy, this is the stage where light and clarity are brought forth. A point at which, once old, existing patterns have been broken and previous assumptions dissolved, the alchemist can start to craft from a blank slate, a tabula rasa. If you think about this in modern terms, this is brainstorming without constraints.

As an alchemist, a creator, an entrepreneur, a product development team, or a thought leader, this stage is where you can start to create something that your customers not only didn't have before, but something they didn't even know was possible prior to this moment. It doesn't have to be gigantic or seismic, but it does need to be some thing, some thought, some feature, some point of reference, that they didn't even realize was possible up to this moment in time.

Albedo is the birthing stage. The birthing that naturally comes after the vacuum left by the Nigredo conceptualizing. When you are done with Nigredo, you have an empty space, and filling that space is what Albedo is all about. It's the creation that comes after the emptying. It's the new rule that fills the space by letting go of the old rule.

WHY ALBEDO?

We typically all know intuitively that part of the innovation process is to come up with something new. So, what's so unique about the Albedo stage inside Synaptic Alchemy? It's a good question: "why don't we all just come up with the next iPod, digital camera, or Netflix?" There are two pieces for us to think about when it comes to Albedo that make it uniquely distinct from traditional brainstorming:

1.) The new ideas birthed from Albedo MUST fill the void of the old rules that were identified in the Nigredo stage.

2.) Birthed ideas must have the chance of growing up and becoming something more than just ideas.

If you think about typical innovation sessions, they generate all sorts of ideas that range from just minor movements away from the traditional, to copies of ideas/products/features that already exist, to harebrained thoughts. And while at times unbridled creativity is good, constraints can provide the walls that allow for the creative impulse to bounce around and magnify, enhancing creative focus.

Albedo is a form of controlled chaos. It resembles childbirth more than it does Chaos Theory, although you may notice aspects of each embedded in the Albedo process.

Let's take a deeper look at why those two points above are a crucial differentiator when it comes to the Albedo birthing process of Synaptic Alchemy.

- **Must fill the void of Old Rules:** That's point number one. Traditional brainstorming sessions, coming up with new idea sessions, birthing of new products, typically start without ever thinking about what the old rules are that need to be broken.

This usually happens when the mandate is to "innovate," and the process is "be creative." This typically unguided process of creativity can yield a wide range of ideas that are relatively shallow. Think about the famous adage from Henry Ford, "if I had asked people what they wanted, they would have said faster horses." If we are just generally looking for new ideas, we tend to look at improving old ones—not necessarily getting rid of old ones.

This is why forcing the New process to stay within the constraints of replacing the Old process is key.

- **Can It Grow Up:** The ability to use constraints to magnify creative focus is very different than traditional thought processes. Usually we see constraints as a negative, they lock us in. However, the concept of looking at constraints as a way to magnify the power of what you DO have access to is unique. Taking an idea and forcing it to exist within current constraints is the key. This step is not about thinking outside the box. This step is about thinking about being able to execute with constraints. I know I'm going to get a ton of pushback on this. I'm not saying that there isn't a place for highly creative 'let's think about anything that is possible' ideas. Those type of pie in the sky brainstorms are wonderful in the appropriate context. Usually in the Nigredo stage. But here in Albedo, it is about dedication to viability and the ability to grow the idea.

Ideas themselves are a dime a dozen. Everyone (and I mean everyone) has interesting (even great) ideas. The ability to take an idea from the heavens and imprint it on the ground is what this point is all about.

Google X - The Moonshot Factory[39] is all about generating new ideas, hence the name. They do, however, have a process that determines which crazy idea they will fund, i.e. which ideas have a chance at moving from the idea infancy stage to the prototype concept toddler stage to the 0.1 version initial product stage of growing up. And they ARE designed to explore extreme ideas.

So why Albedo? Because we need to birth some New Rules from the destruction of the Old Rules. And we need a recipe to guide us along the new and wild path of birthing ideas.

THE ALBEDO MINDSET

Your mindset is the foundation to all future success. The way you think of things, the way you perceive the world around you, and the way you decide to respond makes all the difference. Yes, there are a ton of steps that you need to execute to get from where you are to success, but without the right mindset you might as well not even start. Just recall the last time you attempted something, anything, with a mindset that was negative: a new job, a diet, exercise, learning an instrument, or figuring out a technology. It probably didn't go well. Deciding and committing to the new Synaptic Alchemical mindset IS the cornerstone to turning ideas into gold.

Each of the steps in the Alchemical Transformation: Nigredo, Albedo, Rubedo, carry with them their own mindset. The mindset of Nigredo is to uncover the old rules that we take for granted.

When it comes to Albedo, you'll adopt a mindset of discovery. A way of looking at things as if there were new trade routes to follow, new trails to explore, and new experiences just waiting to blossom. The mindset of Albedo is all about birthing and creating something that wasn't there before.

One of the most interesting Synaptic Alchemists I've had the pleasure of engaging with is Dave Asprey. Dave is the founder, creator and visionary of Bulletproof. We met when we both attended the Wharton MBA program, which created a space for rigorous analytical study as well as a creative soup from which our entire class grew. Knowing Dave, you understand quickly that he is an alchemist at heart as he always explores creation. Although he may not have known it at the time, when Bulletproof Coffee (a recipe for a frothy clean-energy coffee that has become the toast of Silicon Valley) was invented, Dave was completely consumed with the Albedo mind.

Bulletproof coffee was inspired when he was in Nepal and had tasted a tea made with yak-butter. Yep, yak-butter. Taking yak-butter infused tea and handcrafting a coffee that is now sold in locations all over the country, including Whole Foods, takes creativity and seeing something that didn't exist before. Birthing a concept that we didn't even know was possible. That's Albedo in its purest form.

Although he may not have had a single clear Old Rule in mind to replace, he was in fact replacing several. His Albedo creation mindset evolved from the creative destruction mindset of the following:

1. Coffee & Butter don't go together

2. Coffee by itself isn't an energy sustaining breakfast

3. People in the U.S. won't accept adding butter to coffee

4. All coffee roasts are the same

5. You can't get healthier by adding more fat to your morning

And many others. That's the gift of being an alchemist, either explicitly or implicitly. You think in terms of a chain of processes, from old rule (Nigredo) to new rule (Albedo). That is the alchemy of Bulletproof.

As we discussed in the "Why Albedo" section, this is not just unbridled creativity and completely unfettered exploration, it is the creative process in service to the gap left by the Nigredo process of eliminating or changing old rules.

This is where your Synaptic Alchemy recipe of steps for Albedo comes in:

1.) Pollinate: The process of taking disparate concepts and replanting them in a completely new context.

2.) Germinate: The steps to take the rudimentary elements of a concept and bring them into existence.

3.) Socialize: The activities involved in exposing a concept to other points of view.

A good understanding of these three phases of the discovery process of Albedo and allowing one's mindset to be wrapped by these phases can be seen in a variety of historical players. Continuing to use Amazon as our example, let's take a look at how these steps moved Amazon from just an idea into a tidal force.

1.) Pollinate: With the context of "dissolve an Old Rule" and the old rule being "books need to be sold in stores," while Jeff Bezos was founding Amazon, he explored ideas from many disparate industries. Concepts from drop shipping (when early on Amazon built partnerships with bookstores to supply hard-to-find titles) to factory floor automation techniques, to shipping and delivery business models. All were eventually interwoven into the fabric of Amazon's business.

2.) Germinate: Taking the beginnings of small ideas and providing them the nutrients they need to grow is exactly what Jeff Bezos did when it came to ecommerce. Ideas such as the recommendation engine were given the resources and technological room to grow as they slowly morphed into key components of the Amazon infrastructure.

3.) Socialize: Ideas need a way to meet other ideas and idea makers. That is what Amazon did with Alexa. By investing in startups to build voice-control apps for the Alexa personal assistant, the idea of Alexa, along with its ecosystem, was given not just the nutrients necessary to grow but an ever-expanding social circle.

Looking at these three steps helps to understand the innovation culture that exists at Amazon, especially the creation part of the process. Whether the team at Amazon uses this language as part of the innovation process is irrelevant. The techniques are in place that have allowed them to craft, implement, and distribute the creative component of alchemy.

SMALL IS FAST

There is an overarching mentality in the Albedo phase that "small is good." There are times when unbounded creativity can become so expressive that it looks more like boiling the ocean rather than handcrafting the next stage of an idea.

This is not to say that we want to snuff out big vision. Visionary direction coupled with small daily steps IS key to moving forward with any idea within Synaptic Alchemy. The vision can be as grand as is necessary to create a new future. Since Albedo is a step in the visionary process, it is designed to fill the gap left by jettisoning the old rule. Vision is overarching. Albedo is about creating a new rule within the entire vision.

We were probably eight or nine years old as a company. My old company was doing very well securing customers for our second opinion offering. We had determined what we thought was the best process, created software to implement, test and deliver that process, and were consistently talking to our customers about what they needed and attempted to match that with what we provided. We were doing the blocking and tackling of business.

However, our innovation process had become stepwise. We would do one incremental thing to improve our service. Sometimes that increment would be to improve our software just a fraction. One of the tasks we dug into was allowing our customer service reps to work remotely rather than onsite at our offices. We did that to ensure that we could manage any emergencies, from office fires to earthquakes. Definitely something that we needed to have, but not visionary.

Albedo showed up in a very interesting way in our lives. We truly relied on human hands many times in our process. Whether those hands were in sending faxes, or reading medical records, or applying traditional medial guidelines to medical questions. Our software essentially augmented the human part of the process without ever thinking through why we were doing it. That was the Nigredo part. Why is a person doing this thing or that? That was the old rule that eventually was disintermediated.

That's when Albedo appeared, all dressed up. The new rule, the new small is fast part was to take one very small activity (something as simple as faxing) and let the computers do that instead of the humans.

It seems small now. But at the time our vision was to automate anything that would benefit from automation. That was the overarching vision. One Albedo piece was to computerize faxing.

That's the whole point of Albedo. You want to be able to cycle through the Pollination -> Germination -> Socialization triplet as quickly as possible. Because that is what gives you the feedback you need to know which little seedling ideas to feed and grow and which were just fanciful notions.

POLLINATION

Most of the time when we think about the word pollinate we think of flowers. Or maybe agriculture. Or the natural world of trees, fruits and plants. But pollination, specifically, cross-pollination, has been a staple in the business world for quite some time. Cross-pollination is the concept of combining things from different areas to potentially come up with non-obvious solutions to problems. Cross-pollination involves combining ideas that already exist to, essentially, repurpose these combinations.

On the other hand, pollination is not about implementing existing ideas in new ways like cross-pollination (although that is a valuable skill to hone). Pollination is about taking the seeds of an idea and firmly planting them in the ground to see if they will grow. And remember, when it comes to Synaptic Alchemy and Albedo, this pollination is to replace the old rules that we are disintegrating through Nigredo.

Remember, many of the ideas, concepts and products that we plant in the ground will not grow. They won't even start to sprout. That's fine. In fact, that is what we want. In my last company, one of our core principles was "Fail, Forward, Fast." It meant, try all sorts of low-cost concepts and let them fail. Let the customers shrug their shoulders. Let the technology team show you how it can't be done. Let the operations team, the government affairs team, the … blank … team stop new ideas in their tracks. All the ways an idea can't flourish is fine. But for now, we want to plant as many seeds as we can.

There are many techniques that have been cultivated from business, social sciences, and public policy that provide ways to start the pollination process. You'll see a couple of these in the next sections. The important part is to keep in mind that pollination is about planting without an attachment to what the plant (i.e. idea) will look like when it grows up.

With that in mind, let's take a look at two of the many processes that are available to pollinate ideas in Albedo.

Divergence / Convergence

There is nothing new about the cognitive approaches of divergent and convergent thinking. In fact, it was in 1956 that the psychologist J.P. Guilford coined the terms convergent and divergent thinking. The language and concepts behind the best way to approach new ideas or innovation has been well understood for quite some time.

However, many people haven't really done a deep dive into HOW they can best use these two mindsets to innovate.

There are several adjectives that describe both thinking processes.

Convergent thinking: linear, systematic, narrowing, point solutions, focused, why?

Divergent thinking: matrix, relational, expanding, multiple factors, heuristic, why not?

While it is beyond the scope of this book to do a complete deep dive into the details and steps involved in operating a divergent-to-convergent innovation process, there are some unique characteristics that apply within Synaptic Alchemy.

The first is that the divergence/convergence process is not a simple one-time thing. You don't go through this process once and "phew, I'm glad that's over." No, it is a cycle that you will loop through many, many times. Many times, to think through the same concept and many times amongst competing or complementary concepts.

Secondly, as mentioned previously, in the Synaptic Alchemy framework, this is not a creative free-for-all. The divergence/convergence approach in the Albedo phase is within the context of the vacuum left by a good Nigredo process in which you've uncovered old rules that need a complete rework.

Lastly, there is a recipe to this puzzle and certain personalities are better at different parts of the recipe. This is not to say that any one personality is better at one job or another. It just means that different people will bring different expertise to the playing field. For example, individuals who are better at problem solving and finding the holes in a concept will be best suited to the convergence task, while those who are good at creating new, out-of-the-ordinary ideas will be best suited to the divergence task.

Let's take a minute and see what this looks like in real life.

This is something that the team at CID, my last company, did over and over again. Sometimes it was easy. Sometimes, it was excruciatingly difficult. Sometimes it led us to fertile green pastures, and sometimes we would spend hours chasing our own tails with nothing to show for it. Nonetheless, we did the work and eventually came up with more innovative paths.

Divergence

You always start with divergence. This is because that is where you'll generate a volume of ideas. This is where you generate ideas without going too deep into their implementation, and definitely without trying to kill ideas because they won't work. You are trying to expand your thought process, again within the walls of your Nigredo old rule.

We certainly generated ideas at CID. We had plenty of people in senior management (myself included) who could come up with all sorts of wild ideas. A bunch of them only made sense to us, or in some world completely different than the world our customers lived in. At first you would think, "what a waste of time," and occasionally I thought that as well. But it wasn't a waste of time. It allowed us to generate proposals that we wouldn't otherwise have thought of if we censored ourselves and just focused on problem solving.

A key point when you are in divergence is to not get attached to any given suggestion or thought. That's actually a key tool in the Alchemical Toolkit: "Don't Get Attached to Outcome."

We all get attached to our own ideas. Of course, they are OUR ideas. And it is really, really difficult to let go of our own creation. But coming up with ideas without the need to be right, to have them designated as the chosen path, or to fall in love with someone else's idea is key to allowing the divergent thinking process to flow freely. There are many different recipes to encourage divergent thinking, none of them THE recipe. All recipes that generate ideas that work for you and your team are legitimate. There are some recipes that have stood the test of time, but having A recipe is the point.

Convergence

So now you have a bunch of good, bad, crazy, conservative ideas all sitting around in a big think soup waiting for the next step. What's the next step? Well, as you may have guessed, the next step is convergence. Going from generating a large number of options to selecting a few that truly have the chance of moving on from pollination and surviving germination.

Often, we think that convergence means picking the ONE idea that WILL be the RIGHT idea. That's not the best way to go about the process. In fact, if you could pick the winner at this point, why didn't you just start out that way?

The convergence step in Synaptic Alchemy has a couple of iterations. The first is to say No. To find ideas that just won't make it through germination. It doesn't mean picking the one Yes, it means finding the obvious No's.

You'll need metrics in place to screen out ideas that just can't germinate. Maybe those metrics are financial (e.g. this idea will require $50MM in R&D and our budget is $5MM), or maybe they are customer focused (customers have told us over and over again that they won't buy in this way, etc.). The No screen is vital. It is the part of convergence that should be decided prior to the divergence process. Having a set or criteria for the convergence path is essential.

Now that we've whittled the think soup so that the no's are out of the way, we can get to the ideas that are maybe's. They may not get caught in the No screen, but they are close. They have no wiggle room for error or for germinating a little slowly or in a different fashion. Those ideas may need to get cut as well.

We are finally left with a few Yeses. These are the ideas that have passed from divergence and survived the screen of pollination. You may have the ability to force rank these ideas and shepherd several of them into the germination process. That is my recommendation. Don't attempt to pick one winner at this point. Let several of your ideas take root in the germination process and flower from there. The winner, the point solution, will make itself apparent.

A BETTER QUESTION

"A Better Question Is More Important Than the Right
Answer
Because Usually
It's the Right Answer to The Wrong Question"
—Steven Cardinale

Questions: They are how we think. Questions: They are part of our cognitive structure and how we reason about the world around us. Questions: They are the bedrock of our decision making. We make an inordinate number of decisions every single day. By some estimates, we make approximately 35,000 decisions each day[40]. Most of these decisions are not explicit, conscious well-reasoned choices, but more semi-automatic decisions about trivial parts of our day. In fact, when you think about it, every time you make a choice (i.e. decide), you are asking a question, if not out loud then certainly in the quietness of your subconscious. Simple decisions like "should

I get up or hit the snooze button?" More complicated decisions like "do I need to stay late at the office?" Long term decisions like "how much of my paycheck should I save for retirement?"

Since we are so comfortable asking ourselves questions every single day, some 35,000 times, why do we like to come to closure so quickly? Achieving closure equals answering questions, not asking them. You've heard the old phrase, "stop answering my question with a question." But what if the question stack (one question built upon another, with each question containing more insight and moving towards a greater goal) is the golden goose? What if a question stack is the way to innovate and pollinate something new: Some new creation?

We like to come to closure, to answer questions, because it feels like we are moving forward when we do. When we are asking questions we are diverging, giving ourselves more to think about, and that takes a significant amount of cognitive effort. Then there is the non-trivial task of ensuring that the questions we are asking are on topic and valuable, building on prior questions and not taking us off track. Phew, that is a ton of energy. Might as well just choose rather than ask more questions. Right?

Wrong. Questions are how we create. Questions are how we move into the unknown and produce fuel for the divergence mindset of pollination in Albedo. Asking great questions is a key to unlocking the creation process. The question is: How do I ask a Better Question?

That can take practice and a beginner's mind. In Zen Buddhism, this concept is known as Shoshin,[41] which refers to having an open mind free of previous constraints and assumptions. A better question is one that continues to dive deeper into the underlying motivations of the original question until an atomic unit of causality is discovered.

Asking a better question is similar to the engineering discipline of root cause analysis (RCA), but done with Shoshin and a focus on expanding the universe of possibilities, i.e. diverging. An in-depth exploration of Shoshin, RCA and techniques to discover a better question is beyond the scope of this book. However, it is imperative that you develop a finely tuned questioning muscle on your journey towards becoming a Synaptic Alchemist.

A DIFFERENT POV

The well-known author of five New York Times bestsellers and New Yorker writer Malcolm Gladwell has a book entitled "What the Dog Saw." It is a compilation of 19 articles of Gladwell's from the New Yorker magazine. Although there are three sections of the book that describe various themes, including: Obsessives and Pioneers, Theories and Predictions, and finally Personality and Character, the theme that threads through the writing is that looking at life from a unique and different point of view reveals insights that you would otherwise miss.

I actually do this quite a bit. I will lay down next to my dog and look up at the world. It is really interesting how your house, your couch, your kitchen looks when you gaze up at them through the eyes of your dog. Try it someday. Get yourself about one or two feet off the ground and just look around. You'll notice all sorts of things that you otherwise would not see.

That is a staple of innovation, seeing through someone else's eyes. Or walking a mile in someone else's shoes. However you word it, being able to get into another point of view usually will give you insights that you didn't have before.

Insights like: What time could this be done? AM/PM? Day of Week, Month? Always on? With accelerators? Does time matter? Should we be doing this in a recession? (Maybe that's good). What's the trajectory of the future (are things expected to get easier or harder)? Who are the stakeholders? What do they think?

On and on. There are so many ways to look at an idea.

The first thing you need to do is list all of the people and organizations that will interact with your idea. Everything from customers to suppliers to politicians to legal experts. This is where the divergent part of pollination comes into play. Write out every single time someone touches your idea or product. Start with the people or companies who produce the parts, think about how it gets to customers (distribution), then about the people who sell the product or deliver it to the end customer, and then finally to the customer.

This was a very interesting exercise at my last company. We did second opinions for medical procedures. Who exactly were our customers? Were they the other doctors that were receiving the second opinions? Were they the patients themselves? If an attorney was involved, were they the customer? What about the insurance company paying for the second opinion?

As it turned out, we had many customers. Well, actually many stakeholders in our business, because so many people cared about the finished product (including the government, since we were in a regulated industry we had to report to government officials) that we didn't have one end customer.

I remember trying to put on the glasses of each of our stakeholders. To think like an MD and try and understand what an MD cared about. Then to think like a patient and try and understand what a patient cared about. And on and on. Eventually we did speak to each of our stakeholders to understand what was important to them. Each conversation gently nudged different aspects of the business.

That's what a different POV is all about. It is about nudging. Nudging you in a slightly different way so that you see the world through a new pair of eyes.

Marcel Proust is famously quoted as saying:

"The real voyage of discovery consists, not in seeking new landscapes, but in having new eyes."

—Marcel Proust

Isn't that what a different POV is all about?

GERMINATION

In agriculture, germination is when the seedling starts to grow and exits dormancy. That is such a great analogy to the growth path of new ideas. Once ideas have become pollinated, they are ready to take on the next step of growth. Maturing from the soil of experimentation and ideation and beginning their growth path towards adulthood.

Germination can be extremely dependent on external conditions. An idea that has started to sprout will need the right conditions and support to truly take root. Those external conditions both can nourish as well as put external stress factors on the new idea. This is when the group of ideas that come from the divergence / convergence cycle begin to get whittled away and when only the strongest survive.

I've been here many times in my life. When my entrepreneurial instincts have had to give way to the truth of external factors. Those factors have been everything from the ability to finance an idea, to customer adoption, industry standards, and governmental approvals.

Let me say, right now, that moving from a little seed and germinating into an adult idea can be a precarious time. I remember with my previous company having what we thought were unique and innovative ideas. Ideas around delivery. Ideas around transparency. Ideas around pricing. And then those ideas didn't survive the germination process. Customers told us that "we just don't buy like this," and there went an idea around delivery. When it came to transparency, the type that we thought was important, I've had the government tell me, "we just can't have the entire industry collect that data," and there went a transparency idea. And then there was the customer that said, "my accounting systems won't let me take that type of discount," and there went a new way of pricing.

All great ideas. But as you've heard before, "ideas are a dime a dozen." There is so much truth to that statement that it's difficult to overstate. Because ideas alone really are not worth $0.01. Now ideas that have come to life through Nigredo, been pollinated through the first step of Albedo, and start to germinate—those ideas are starting to see the light of day, and they are becoming the foundational soup that will eventually yield gold.

You now know that germination is the process of using external conditions to either strengthen or eliminate ideas from pollination. Let's start exploring the recipes in germination.

SWOT

Strengths, Weaknesses, Opportunities, Threats. If you earned your MBA or are a student of business, I am sure you have heard of this exercise. This is the only time that we'll directly use a well-established business concept in this book. Although many of the ideas in business recycle and re-establish themselves in other formats, and the ideas of innovation within Synaptic Alchemy may feel familiar, SWOT analysis is one of our core tools.

SWOT Analysis is credited to Albert Humphrey, who developed the approach at the Stanford Research Institute back in the 1960s and early 1970s. It has been around for a while and is well established.

While a complete course on SWOT analysis is beyond the scope of this book, we'll go through a top line review of the concepts and how those concepts fit within Synaptic Alchemy and Albedo. You'll take the outcome of your SWOT analysis and use it in the Socialization phase of Albedo.

S for Strengths

This represents the forces that already align with your idea. For example, it might be new legislation coming down the pipe that your idea can help implement. That would be governmental alignment as a strength. Or it could be customer demand. When customers are clamoring for something this idea delivers, well, you won't have to worry about demand generation and that is definitely a strength. Or it could be proprietary, defensible technology that you already own. That too is counted as a strength.

Strength is represented by the installation of internal traits that gives your idea the water and nutrients it needs to grow and sustain itself. The process of coming up with strengths is straightforward. You start documenting all the financial, governmental, physical, human, natural, technological, intellectual and infrastructure resources that you have access to. These become the soil that you can draw on to grow your idea. The more powerful your strengths, the stronger the root system of your idea.

Here is where it gets tricky. You can't delude yourself. YOU can't decide that a strength is a strength. It has to be considered a strength from an outside source. So, if you think your technology is great, but someone from the outside (e.g. an investor) would argue otherwise (e.g. it is easily replicated, or other firms have the same tech, or it is not proprietary) then it is not a strength. It requires an impartial set of eyes to look at your strengths. If not, then maybe the strengths you see are not real strengths. We're looking for strengths that provide your idea a real competitive advantage. This is where the Art part of the Synaptic Alchemist comes in.

In our little tech example in the previous paragraph, it is not that the tech is not a strength, the strength might be that you have already built the technology foundation you need (i.e. an infrastructure strength), but you wouldn't consider technology that is not proprietary a technology strength.

W for Weakness

I'm sure you can guess how we look for weaknesses. They seem like they are the opposite of strengths. But let's think about weaknesses for a moment. A weakness in an internal characteristic that doesn't just hinder growth; a weakness is a characteristic that could eventually stop growth altogether, or a characteristic that could be exploited by an external force (e.g. the market, a competitor, etc.) that could significantly impair the capacity of your ideas to grow.

This is a different way of thinking about the W in SWOT than is traditional: Weaknesses as risks that either must be shored up or mitigated away. The Synaptic Alchemy way of looking at the weakness component of SWOT is: Weakness = Unmitigated Risk.

I'm not saying that the traditional analytical framework of looking at weakness as a lack of resources (e.g. financing, physical, human, etc.) is not worth considering, it is. But rather, looking at weakness as a measure of curable or mitigatable risk is the unique perspective of the alchemist. I know this sounds a bit academic, so let's take a look at a real-world example.

When I was running my company, we worked in a market that had many governmental regulations. Part of our strength was being able to comply with the government regulations (which required privacy protection, reporting, licensing, etc.) in a very efficient manner.

Being able to comply with the government was a strength for us. A weakness for us was Legislative Risk. The regulations could, and did, change on a dime. What was in a bill depended on who was sponsoring the bill and what their agenda was, and then what other legislators would add on to the bill. It was exhausting trying to keep up with all the potential legal changes that we might have to comply with. Our legislative risk was really a weakness of the business as a whole.

When we came up with new ideas, we would have to grade them on how much additional legislative risk the idea would create. If we had a new idea to allow doctors to adopt new medical research, we had to make sure that the research they were using was approved by the government. And if the government changed what research was allowed, we would have to spin on a dime to make the changes.

This Weakness = Unmitigated Risk equation works especially well when it comes to idea differentiation. The ability to look at your ideas in terms of how much additional risk they either have individually or add to the organization as a whole is vital to deciding on their SWOT value.

O for Opportunities

When looking at opportunities, traditional SWOT analysis looks at external factors that give you an upper hand. However, looking at opportunities through the lens of the germination phase of Albedo, we tilt our vision slightly and start to look at external factors that can be capitalized on using your idea. Not just to benefit from, but something that your new idea will allow you to benefit from at 10x.

An opportunity is not just an external factor that is available to anyone, but an external factor that your idea can leverage and multiply. It is this 10x multiple that really drives the idea opportunity set.

Let's work through an example. Cerulli Associates predicts that over the next 25 years, a total of $48 trillion in wealth will be transferred from Baby Boomers to their heirs and to charity (out of a total of $68.4 trillion for all generations greater than

50 years old).[42] That is an opportunity for almost all businesses in the financial advising industry and in a traditional SWOT analysis would represent an opportunity to explore.

However, from a Synaptic Alchemy point of view, unless the idea that we are trying to germinate can credibly capitalize on that huge shift in assets in a way that is 10x greater than the competition, then it might be a market opportunity, but not an idea opportunity.

Let's take this analysis a little further. Research estimates the growth of the Robo-Advisory section of wealth management to be around 47% year over year (as of 2020).[43] That growth will move the industry from $240 billion in assets to over $2.5 trillion in assets by 2023. That is the type of opportunity that nimble firms who can capitalize on it can truly include in their O for opportunity.

So, just because there is an external factor that creates opportunities for everyone, doesn't mean that the prospects for your Albedo idea or concept can benefit from those opportunities. Global opportunities are just that, global, everyone benefits. Albedo Germination Idea Opportunities are individual to the idea. The O part of SWOT in Synaptic Alchemy shifts the point of view from the macro to the micro and from the micro to the singular … to the idea.

T for Threats

The threats to an idea have a similar feel to the opportunities segment of SWOT. There can be external pressures that are felt by everyone and that can create existential threats to business as easily as ideas. The external part of the equation is important. Threats come from the outside, and when it comes to the germination stage, not just outside a business or team, but outside the idea itself.

The difference between a threat and an opportunity in Albedo SWOT analysis is that you have to try to discover and capitalize on an opportunity, however, threats come right to your front door whether you are on the lookout for them or not.

Let's take a modern look at an external threat that may exist for the organization but not necessarily the idea (which is the frame of reference for Synaptic Alchemy).

Google (Alphabet) is well positioned as the leader in search with 91.7% of the market[44]. With such a dominant market share, and with the next player Bing at 2.75% and Yahoo at 1.7%, you would think that it would be difficult to really be able to chip away at Google's superiority. And if you were thinking directly in the search market, the search for terms and ideas, you'd be right.

But that is not where the immediate threat to Google comes from. The biggest threat might be Facebook and Amazon. Facebook allows searching in a social context and Amazon offers the ability to search and sort for products with reviews and recommendations.

Consequently, ideas relevant to Google must take into account the external threat of Facebook or Amazon as a search platform and truly handle the threats that these non-search companies represent as they expand search functionality.

ROUGH PROTOTYPING

When you think of the word rough, what comes to mind? Does the feeling of the bumpy texture of sandpaper bubble up? Or do the unpolished, stream-of-consciousness sentences and paragraphs of a first draft essay appear in your mind.

Either way, when talking about the roughness of a prototype in the germination phase of Albedo, we are referring to a model or mock-up of an idea without worrying about if it fits the polished idea of the final product. That is because in the germination phase there is no final product target to aim for.

There are two important mindsets to understand during rough prototyping:

1.) Don't Attach to Outcome

2.) Fail Forward Fast

These are two highly regarded principles of the Alchemist's Tool Kit.

The first, "don't attach to outcome," is vital in rough prototyping because when you are prototyping there shouldn't be an outcome that you are looking to emulate. If you are too worried about what your prototype SHOULD look like or act like, you won't be able to be creative enough to develop what your prototype WILL look like or act like. You'll be spending all of your focus on trying to hit an elusive goal. Let it go. What you should focus on is prototyping to learn, prototyping to experiment, prototyping to generate ideas and discoveries.

The second, "fail, forward, fast," is core to prototyping. In running CID, my team absolutely had the mindset of "progress over perfection." We are not taught that failing is acceptable. Whether that comes from school or the corporate hierarchy, failure is looked down upon. Changing what it means to fail is crucial. I'm not talking about bet the business kind of decisions that lead to either success or demise. I'm talking about quick, small experiments that provide vital clues to how an idea can and will germinate.

In 2016, Jeff Bezos, CEO of e-commerce juggernaut Amazon, famously called Amazon "the best place in the world to fail"[45] in his letter to shareholders. He wrote:

"One area where I think we are especially distinctive is failure. I believe we are the best place in the world to fail (we have plenty of practice!), and failure and invention are inseparable twins. To invent you have to experiment, and if you know in advance that it's going to work, it's not an experiment."

—Jeff Bezos

Prototyping is designed to draw out the characteristics of your idea as it matures. Prototyping is designed as a way to build parts of the plane while it is flying.

These two mindsets are so critical in this stage of the ideation process. Not worrying about what the outcome will look like, and not being afraid to fail.

This mindset IS a key competitive advantage. A secret of sorts. And being fully committed to the mindset itself is vital to your alchemical exploration.

SOCIALIZATION

We all know what a product launch is. We've seen them in action. Apple is legendary when it comes to product launches. The iPhone 4 sold 1.7 million units in three days. The first iPad itself sold 300,000 WiFi-only units on its first day in 2010 and sold nearly 7.5 million units that year. The Rubik's Cube (yep that crazy looking little square toy) was launched internationally in 1980 and by 1982 had sold 100 million units.

We have an idea of what a product launch is and why it matters. It matters because it allows us to decide if our audience is going to love the product, with all of its fancy features, colorful marketing, and brilliant execution, or if it is just ... meh ... if it is irrelevant. Let me be honest. I hate being irrelevant. General Eric Shinseki, former chief of staff for the US Army, is quoted as saying:[46]

> "If you don't like change, you're going to like irrelevance even less"

— General Eric Shinseki

It's a great quote that cuts right to the heart of the matter. Irrelevance can take a technically or operationally or ...ly (fill in the blank) product and render it DOA. According to Harvard Business School professor Clayton Christensen, 30,000 new products are introduced each year, and 95% of them fail.[47] I am sure there are some failures that are due to the product itself. There are some that are due to placement or promotion. But I'm also sure that the majority of those failures are because the product was irrelevant to the audience it was designed for.

It is easy to see, after the fact, that a product was just not going to capture the imagination of the customer and would end up on the scrap heap of innovation. Whether it was Cheetos flavored Lip Balm designed to compete with Chapstick, Blistex and Burt's Bees, or Coors Rocky Mountain ... wait for it ... Sparkling Water to compete with Pellegrino and Perrier, these misfires seem obvious in the rearview mirror.

We are all viscerally aware of product launches, but what about idea launches. It is at the ideation stage, and specifically the end of the Albedo stage, where the misfires could have been observed faster and at a lower cost. Remember the Fail, Forward, Fast strategy? Socialization is like a megaphone for that process, and something that is vital to innovation.

Let's take a look at the three steps of socialization within the Albedo phase of Synaptic Alchemy.

ALL DRESSED UP

You know what it is like to get all dressed up, to find your best clothes, put on your finest outfit, find the most luxurious attire and get ready to go out. But have you ever wondered why we get dressed up in the first place? Why do we spend the time, money and energy to put on our Sunday Best, or get "dressed up to the nines," (which, by the way, is a phrase, thought to reference the Nine Worthies or the nine Muses, said to have originated from Scotland[48]), or find a way to end up "putting' on my top hat, Tyin' up my white tie, Brushin' off my tails" (lyrics from a song written by Irving Berlin for the 1935 film Top Hat[49])?

That's a good question, and it may surprise you that economists[50] and evolutionary biologists[51] have studied this phenomenon and, although they may differ significantly on the details, the core motivation they identify is consistent, at least through our Synaptic Alchemy lens. We get dressed up, put on our best outfit, and present our best image to others so we can communicate (i.e. signal) our value.

When it comes to evolutionary biology, that value is our fitness as a mate. When it comes to economics, we get dressed up to signal to others that whatever we have is valuable. Valuable means relevant, which is what socialization is all about in the context of ideation and the Albedo phase of Synaptic Alchemy.

Just think about education. What is one of the major reasons we go to universities? Well, obviously, one is to accrue knowledge. The higher quality the knowledge the better. The other is for the certification. The degree which is a signal to future employers of our capabilities. That's why we are so brand sensitive, certainly within the United States.

Brand = Signal

&

Signal = Relevance

Taking this principle of signaling theory and applying it to ideation—especially when an idea is young and forming as it is in Albedo—gives us some direction as to whether the idea will be relevant to the world once the idea is fully baked.

An irrelevant idea, no matter how well conceived, will be starved for attention. And attention provides the nutrients and is the currency that allows ideas to prosper and grow.

So, what does it mean to get your idea all dressed up? Well, it is pretty close to what it means for you to personally get all dressed up. You start to think about how others will perceive you and how you can get noticed (i.e. be relevant) when you are out in the world.

For ideas, that may mean creating presentations that show the idea in action. It may mean creating mood or vision boards so that customers can understand what the idea will mean to them when it is finally ready for a full launch. It may mean spreadsheets showing how wonderful your idea looks in its financial tux and tails.

There are many ways to dress up an idea and have it ready for a public presentation. This is why at times going out to find financing is such a good exercise, whether you secure funding for your idea or not. It forces you to dress up your idea and understand what the idea looks like through someone else's eyes.

There is a tool in the Alchemical Tool Kit that expresses this exactly. "It's Not About You." In a nutshell it means that having to look at your idea through someone else's glasses is one of the key exercises to see if it is relevant to others.

Being relevant is what socialization is all about. Get dressed to the nines and let's see what type of attention shows up.

THE GRAND ENTRANCE

You certainly can't be all dressed up and then suddenly have nowhere to go. Although that may have made its way into the internet culture as a meme,[52] we definitely don't want our ideas to be looking their best and signaling they are ready for prime time and then hear crickets.

This is what the Grand Entrance is all about. It is about finding an audience that is ready, willing and able to meet your grand idea head on. And once you have found that audience, it is about making the right entrance, creating the right noise, and making the right introductions.

We are in the socialization segment of Albedo. Our idea is now starting to make the rounds and touch the outside world. We are not quite ready to launch and scale at this point (that is what happens when we move to Rubedo); what we're looking for is feedback and the first glimpses of what an outside market really thinks about our new Synaptic Alchemical idea.

Since we have gotten our idea all dressed up and ready to make an entrance, it is time to start to think about ... how DO we make a grand entrance? This is not a product launch, this is an idea launch, a concept launch, a get-to-know-this-idea launch. Sure, there may be prototypes, and demos, and discussions, but we are still in the ideation phase.

When you are going to make a grand entrance, it is important to understand for whom you are making the entrance. For example, if, for all intents and purposes, you make a grand entrance as a new consumer good (e.g. the newest laundry detergent) but your entrance is to a conference room full of engineers, you are probably going to get a ... meh ... reaction.

Knowing your audience and then being able to capture their attention is essential to a successful grand entrance. With that in mind, let's take a deeper dive into what attention really is and how to best grab ahold of some of it.

PAYING ATTENTION

Can you remember the last time you were completely obsessed by something? When you just couldn't take your eyes off what you were doing, what you were focused on, what you were paying attention to. We have all had that experience when we dedicated our focus to a very specific task at hand; when you finally paid attention to something important and stopped looking at all the superfluous noise in your environment; when you truly understood that what you were looking at was WORTH looking at above all else.

This is what it means to pay attention. What true Synaptic Alchemists strive to accomplish is to get people to pay attention.

Attention is the new currency of the digital world. Attention can be monetized with advertising, sponsorships, or premium content. Attention can be directed and shaped. And attention can be focused to present new ideas that have never before seen the light of day.

We do not really think about an audience having to pay to see something. But that's exactly what they do. They PAY attention. And the currency that they are paying with is their ATTENTION. It is critical to think about attention in this way. Because it allows you to see that your audience is making a choice to spend their time and focus on something specific. If your grand entrance or your idea is not worth it, they will pay their attention to something else.

As a Synaptic Alchemist, you are deciding where your attention should be directed on a consistent basis. In fact, as you take your alchemical journey you will find yourself quickly assessing what is worth spending your attention on and not buying intellectual or emotional junk food with your attention currency. This is something that your audience does implicitly. They decide where to spend their attention currency.

VALUING ATTENTION CURRENCY

On average, as human beings we don't tend to think of putting an intentional conscious value on our attention. We tend to think attention is infinite and can be easily spent without losing value. "What's one minute on Facebook, or a little bit of time playing video games, or just a quick jaunt down the aisles of the internet. It's my lunch time and I need a break. I'm just killing some time." As people, that is what we tell ourselves. It's a story that allows us to spend our attention currency with abandon. But think about it. Our attention is limited. We all have

- 60 minutes every hour

- 24 hours every day

- 1,440 minutes every day

- 7 days a week

- A little more than 10,000 minutes a week

- Around 40,000 minutes a month

What's a few minutes wasted here and there? It is only time. Right? Wrong.

Your audience will viscerally feel it if your grand entrance, your point of view, your value is not aligned with what is vital in their eyes, and they will quickly decide to spend their attention currency on something else. Whether that means that they will start to check their email, scroll Instagram, or post comments on social media during your presentation, or ignore you completely once they are done with the initial encounter, is not important; what is important is that your grand entrance must entice them to spend their attention on you.

Time and therefore Attention Currency IS the ONLY NON-RENEWABLE RESOURCE.

Since attention currency is non-renewable, as an alchemist you will have to focus on ensuring that your message and your audience's appetite are aligned.

BEHAVIORAL INTENTIONALITY

There are two thought leaders that provide insight into the alignment of your grand entrance—your message—and an audience's attention appetite.

The customer adoption lifecycle model offered by Geoffrey Moore in "Crossing the Chasm" is valuable as a direction for audience discovery. In the adoption lifecycle, Moore discusses five different customer segments: innovators, early adopters, early majority, late majority, laggards. Moore explains:

> "Each group represents a unique psychographic profile—
> a combination of psychology and demographics that
> makes its marketing responses different from those of the
> other groups." —Geoffrey Moore, Crossing the Chasm,
> 3rd Edition

There are many different ways to use demographics and psychographics to understand an audience segment. In Moore's case, each segment sees technology as useful for their own purposes through a different lens. For example, Innovators are intrigued with new technology from a fundamental curiosity standpoint. Their intention is to learn a new technology to expand their technical prowess and satisfy their hunger for innovation; whereas, individuals in the Early Majority are ultimately interested in the practicality of the offering. Their intention is to only engage with products once their efficacy and stability have been proven. These two groups have very different intentions when they finally jump in with both feet.

The hidden intentions of a group (whether you use demographics or psychographics, or both, or some other clustering method) are what lie underneath their purchase decisions and engagement.

The concept of the dissemination of ideas offered by Malcolm Gladwell in "The Tipping Point"[53] can be overlaid on the audience segments identified by Moore. Gladwell's ideas are a perfect starting point to discuss the transmission of ideas across society. He discusses three vital audience accelerators: Connectors, Salesmen & Mavens.

Without going into a deep dive on the concepts in The Tipping Point (which is an ABSOLUTE MUST READ for all aspiring alchemists), each of these personality types share information in a very unique way. For example, Mavens will collect and store the knowledge of new innovations and distribute that knowledge for those able to absorb these innovations.

Joining these two concepts—**adoption segmentation and audience accelerators**—gives us a wonderful framework to understand how to create an entrance that our audience will pay attention to.

By combining Who we are creating an entrance for (their intentions, i.e. adoption segment), and How they behave (their interaction style, i.e. audience accelerator), an alchemist can artfully craft an entrance message designed to capture and hold the audience's attention.

Let me give you a quick example of where I've seen the right grand entrance with the right audience and where I've seen it completely fall on its face.

When I was on the road talking to potential purchasers of my company, there were many investors that were interested but only in a cursory way.

I distinctly remember walking into a very expensive office complete with a large Mahogany table, floor-to-ceiling glass windows overlooking a huge metropolis, and speaking with a senior executive who couldn't care less about my company.

This executive was interested in doing deals 10-100x larger than mine. Why was he taking the meeting, when it was apparent that he wasn't going to part with any of his attention? I'm not sure. Maybe it was because he wanted to see what was coming up in the industry? Maybe it was because someone else asked him to? Whatever the reason, both he and I realized quite quickly that the innovations I was discussing and his attention span were not aligned.

But here's the thing. I got my company all dressed up anyways and made a grand entrance ... to crickets. Lesson learned. He was not part of my audience and I wasn't saying anything that was meaningful to him.

Next time I went to present to another investor, I did more homework. I learned about my audience. I spent the time to get an idea where they were in the adoption lifecycle and what their personality was all about. In fact, it took really getting to understand the motivations (intentions) and personalities (behaviors) of many executives in the transaction to finally make a grand entrance that made a splash, got everyone to pay attention, and eventually created a highly polished partnership and acquisition.

Making your grand entrance can take a significant amount of work. We all think that we're just going to jump in front of an audience and they will clap and cheer for us. Well, it doesn't usually work that way. Audience development, alignment, and interaction so the audience will pay attention is an art, and hopefully, now that you have some Synaptic Alchemy in your bones, one that is a bit more understandable.

LISTEN, LISTEN, LISTEN

You have gotten your idea all dressed and cleaned up and ready to meet your audience. You have determined your audience's segmentation and accelerators and crafted a message that will capture their attention. So now what?

Well ... shut up and listen. I know that can be hard when we have spent all this time preparing our new idea, polishing every facet and sanding every nook and cranny. We become attached. Detachment is one of those tools that all alchemists must constantly attend to. Now that you have their attention, now that you know you are saying something that is aligned with what your audience wants to hear, you just have to listen to them. They will tell you wondrous things if you just open your ears and listen.

However, it is not just listening for listening's sake. It is alchemical listening.

I have been chastised in the past for the following statement. That it is too harsh. Or that it is all about not listening. The statement is:

"Your opinion is the least most important piece of information right now."

Ow. Yep, sounds harsh. And perhaps it is. This language usually comes up when someone is offering me their unsolicited opinion. I don't want it. Opinions are merely stated preferences.

"Chocolate is the best flavor ice cream" is stated as an opinion. "I like Chocolate ice cream best," is the same opinion expressed as a preference. Neither provides an alchemist with what we're looking for. We are looking for language that drives action and decisions. We are looking for **actionable data**.

What then does "Listen, Listen, Listen" mean if you don't want opinions? Well, what we're looking for is something similar to a Net Promoter Score (NPS for short)[54]. The NPS is all about trying to discover if a consumer would spread the word about your product or idea. Not whether they liked it. Not whether they think it should be painted a different color. Only if they would recommend it to a colleague.

As an alchemist you are listening for actions, like:

• I got bored reading at chapter 7.

- I put the book down at page 100 because it was too confusing.

Or you are listening for substitution, like:

- I'd rather keep using my other software/tool/idea right now.

- I already do this with ... (fill in the blank).

That's what we are listening for, one of three things: 1.) Recommendations 2.) Actions 3.) Substitutions

We are not just listening passively. Alchemical listening is quite active. To make that listening active you will have to guide your audience to provide you feedback in a certain way. It is not just a free-for-all in terms of expressing opinions at this point. There is a very intentional process in this listening.

Doing a deep dive in the art of alchemical listening usually requires a good chunk of training. It is similar to martial arts training. You could read a book on how to make a fist, but you need some time sparring in the ring to get a real feel for what it is like in the real world. That's the art of alchemical listening.

ALBEDO ALL WRAPPED UP

You now have a good understanding of some of the tools and mindsets that comprise Albedo. Just by having a framework you are lightyears ahead of your competition. You were introduced to the three steps to igniting an idea: Pollination, Germination & Socialization. All great ideas go through this process, whether their creators are conscious of the steps or not. The more consciously you can attend to these steps the more tools you will have in your toolbox.

Albedo is all about ideation, all about creating the new idea that will take the place of the old idea that was abolished in Nigredo. That is a key distinction between the alchemical ideation process and ideation in traditional innovation. Ideation and brainstorming in the Albedo context is only in service of creating a New Rule where there was an Old Rule that is going to be disintermediated. This type of thinking, replacing the old with the new, is what gives Albedo some of its unique characteristics. The constraints of being in service to Nigredo and to the alchemical transformation itself is what creates the boundaries that ideas can ricochet off to boost velocity during the Albedo phase.

Now that an old rule has been identified, and new rules have been brainstormed to take their place, it is time to breathe

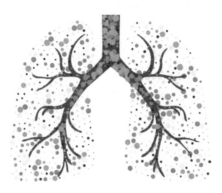

This is the reddening stage, featuring an integration of what took place in the previous stages back into the world. It might sound a bit morbid, since the redness reflects the point when blood and passion enter the alchemist's work. It is really all about taking the purity of the idea from Albedo and translating that pure idea into the flesh, blood and bone of success.

I've heard this called the "messy middle." The mess that occurs at the point in time where you cross the bridge from just a wonderful idea into something real that everyone can hold in their hands. It doesn't just have to be a physical product, it can be virtual, like the moment when a song goes from something in your head and something you play for your friends, to music that is heard around the world. Or the moment when a policy idea starts traversing the legislative system on its way to becoming a law. Or when an idea for a business moves from just being a great idea and starts serving customers at scale.

As Synaptic Alchemists, Rubedo will be the phase where we focus on bringing your big idea to market. This book is concerned with the big picture of alchemy; the alchemy of innovation and the alchemy of ideas. In this section, we'll focus on Rubedo as the mindset of delivering your idea in its completed form to your audience. This Rubedo phase won't focus on demand generation or audience development, even though that is part of delivering your idea to the largest possible audience. That is subject matter for the Synaptic Alchemy of Marketers. In this book, we are focused on the mindset necessary to deliver innovation.

WHY RUBEDO?

When we have the inventor hat on, the idea generation hats of Nigredo and Albedo, we get the luxury of allowing ourselves to create without the guard rails of delivery. However, once an idea is baked and ready to launch to the world in a significant way, we have to change our focus.

This is where we have to decide to move from giving 100% of our attention to the one unique idea and all of its wondrous facets and start focusing on systematizing our idea. That doesn't sound very romantic ... systematizing. Sounds somewhat robotic. Sounds disconnected from the joyous freedom of generating ideas.

But it's not. Just stick with me for a minute and you'll understand why. The idea itself is just an idea. It doesn't live in the real world. It is sort of an abstract. Yes, you may have a prototype, and it may have been introduced to some of society, but the idea itself really needs to be born into the real world. Carl Jung has a wonderful description of Rubedo:

"In the state of 'whiteness' one does not live in the true sense of the word. It is a sort of abstract, ideal state. In order to make it come alive it must have 'blood', it must have what the alchemists called the rubedo, the 'redness' of life."

—Carl Jung

When it comes to ideas, getting them out into the real world, letting our ideas become products, services, policies, or businesses, Rubedo is all about allowing our ideas to emerge from the confines of our creative energies and provide value to the outside world.

In order to do that, our ideas have to scale. Which means having to stop the idea part and switch to the systems part. That is the part that breathes life into ideas. The systems that let our ideas interact with the world.

That is what Rubedo is all about. Building the ecosystem necessary to breathe life into our ideas. Breathing life into an idea feels a lot less robotic than systematizing. But that's just because systematizing represents the tactical steps that you use to spark life. Your systems allow your idea to get into the hands of your audience. If you think systematizing = breathing life into your idea, your mindset will change and so will your focus. Which is what you'll need to do in Rubedo. Change your focus. And what is Why Rubedo.

THE RUBEDO MINDSET

The mindset of Rubedo is very different from the previous phases. You'll move from focusing on a singular idea to a process focus. This can represent a huge shift for many alchemists. You suddenly have to let go of the singular focus on idea and move to the operational focus of systems.

That's the tough part:

Idea -> System

How do you even do that? How do you stop thinking about your creation and start thinking about the processes of producing your creation? Well, that is what we are going to explore in this section. However, there are a couple of caveats.

1.) **You can't fall in love with your creation:** If you are familiar with the Pygmalion myth, where the Greek sculptor Pygmalion carved his ideal woman as a statue and eventually fell in love with his own creation[55], this is what I'm talking about here. You'll need to become dispassionate about the wondrous features of your idea so you can start to think objectively about the process of producing your idea. This is a significant mindset shift that will be required of you. Remember, ideas themselves are a dime-a-dozen. However, a well-executed, produced, and delivered idea is the stuff of gold and legends.

2.) **Stop being the creator and start being the orchestrator:** It is no wonder that only 25% of companies are run by the original entrepreneur / founder after their company's initial public offering.[56] There is a mindset transition that occurs when moving from innovation to production. In the world of the ancient alchemist, you would have come up with a recipe for turning lead into gold, but actually turning large piles of lead into the shiny substance requires much more than just a recipe.

That's why you have to stop being the creator and start being the orchestrator. Bringing your idea to market requires you to build systems that can replicate your idea and deliver it en masse. As author, thought leader and NYU professor Scott Galloway has stated: "Greatness is achieved in the agency of others." This is never truer than in the Rubedo phase of alchemy. Your ability to build systems will rely on working with other systems thinkers. The sculpting phase implicit in Nigredo and Albedo is complete. Now it's time to start orchestrating the delivery systems.

Those two caveats are difficult to manage for many: 1.) Don't fall in love with your creation 2.) Stop being the creator. However, if you don't decide to make this transition, you'll find it extremely difficult, if not impossible, to truly build something worthy of the gold standard.

Building teams to systematize and mass produce the gold that is their ideas is what the great entrepreneurs of lore accomplished. Jeff Bezos no longer personally runs Amazon.com, there are legions of software engineers that manage that. Long before Bill Gates stepped away from Microsoft, he stopped running each individual section of Windows. And even though Elon Musk may at times spend twenty hours a day at the office, he is not hands-on in the factory bending steel for Tesla cars. All of these entrepreneurs transitioned from idea generators to visionary industry captains by relying on the skills of others and simultaneously turning their focus to systems.

DETACHMENT

Core to the systemization required by Rubedo is cultivating a mindset of detachment from the idea itself. As we live through ideation, we become attached to what we are creating. That's a good thing in ideation. It allows us to truly get behind our concepts and shepherd them through the toughest of times. However, with the Pygmalion caveat from the last chapter in mind, we are now past the ideation process and on to pouring our golden idea into molds. This is the detachment point. Detaching is all about letting go of your creation.

When we ideate, we, by design, create a unique one-off solution. You can think of the ideation phase as creating a custom suit designed to perfectly fit each and every customer's needs. The first step in Rubedo, and a critical step, is to let go of the one-of-a-kind idea / invention / policy / business / service that you have created. This can be a difficult mindset shift and I've seen big companies and sophisticated teams stumble at this critical juncture.

Sometimes it is because we fall in love with our creations, sometimes it is because our egos get in the way and still want to hold on and receive the accolades associated with invention, and sometimes it is because we may not be confident in our capabilities in this new world of systemization. Whatever the reason, the transition is a natural and necessary part of the gold casting process.

Geoffrey Moore, author of "Crossing the Chasm" and "Inside the Tornado," provides a compelling outline of why detachment is necessary. Detachment from a customized or bespoke offering is necessary so that your idea can reach scale and become standardized enough to be adopted by the masses. In order to do this, the Synaptic Alchemist must detach from the idea itself.

> "Do anything you can to streamline the creation, distribution, installation, and adoption of your whole product. The more friction you can avoid, the more throughput you can achieve." —Geoffrey Moore, Inside the Tornado

"your focus must be on getting [the customer] that item as

quickly, easily, and cheaply as possible. This means

becoming intensely internally focused on your delivery

capabilities and not letting yourself get distracted by

"secondary" factors such as an individual customer's

particular needs."

—Geoffrey Moore, Inside the Tornado

As our ideas grow and become accepted through the socialization of the Albedo phase, we become attached. However, innovations at the end of the Albedo stage typically are customized to solve a particular problem for a particular cohort of customers. Letting go of the persona of creator, of the ego thrill that comes from birthing a new way of doing things, is precisely what is necessary at this point. Author Ryan Holiday has a book about Stoic philosophy entitled "Ego is the Enemy," which precisely describes how holding on to the persona of creator is the thing you'll have to let go of to get through this phase.

I've been there, in complicated ways and in the simplest of ways. Detaching can be tough. In running my company, I wore a bunch of hats, as all entrepreneurs do when creating a company or expanding into uncharted territory. Some days, I would play the part of Chief Technology Officer, other days I'd change my hat to play COO, and on others I would be working on M&A as a founder/CFO, while still others required the strategic mindset of CEO. In touching the business in so many ways, you can't help but become entwined in the ideas that come out of ideation.

I still remember working on an idea (in fact, the idea in the story at the beginning of this book) that everyone thought was ridiculous. It was software that automated many of the first steps our doctors and our customers' nurses performed. I was coding on planes traveling between clients, programming in hotel rooms awaiting the next meeting, and coming up with prototypes on the fly while pulling ideas out of the air. That is the creative frenzy that can happen when you are in ideation mode. When you are fully engulfed in the Nigredo and Albedo phases of the synaptic storm.

Then something crazy happened. Customers started to buy our products. Small ones, big ones, all sorts of sizes. Of course, I was elated. We were getting market success in the form of product adoption. Sales were happening. Customers were validating the idea. Then customers started to want changes just for them. And we had to say no most of the time. We had to make enhancements that benefited everyone, not just one single customer. But when one customer wanted a button moved here, or a change in process there, unless it was something the market needed, it was a hard no.

That was the hardest part of the entire development lifecycle. We had to stop focusing on all the cool things our product COULD do for one and focus on what our product SHOULD do for all. No more custom code which would make this customer's screen look exactly how they wanted it to look. Suddenly, it was about driving costs down, driving adoption up, and letting go of innovation.

There were many nights when I woke up thinking about how to do more product development. Customize a screen here for customer A, a process there for customer B. It is almost like becoming enchanted by the invention process itself. A kind of inventor madness. That was when something happened that imprinted the value of detachment.

I suddenly let go of developing prototypes and moved team members to build out and maintain the product. Letting go of ideation and moving to leadership (which is a type of orchestration) was key. It is hard to detach. There's a certain grief in it. A certain feeling of loss. Which is why tools and techniques are vital to provide signposts to detach.

Holding on will give you some certainty that you can continue to ideate, but it will close off your idea to most of your audience. Once you've decided that you'd rather be—and are better at—becoming a conductor, you will have the opportunity to move from certainty to curiosity.

RUBE GOLDBERG CURIOSITY

If you are old enough to know what a Rube Goldberg machine[57] is (and if you aren't go Google it, they are really fun), then you will recognize either this image or it will bring back similar images. Rube Goldberg himself was an American cartoonist who intentionally designed overly complicated machines (also known as Rube Goldberg contraptions) to solve simple problems. In this cartoon, "Professor Butts and the Self-Operating Napkin" from 1931, the machine is designed to clean Professor Butts' mouth while he is eating dinner via a process that required 13 steps to complete.

While funny, and never something I'd suggest as a Synaptic Alchemist, the thought process, the creativity, the curiosity around systems, as expressed in these cartoons, is a concept that can give the Synaptic Alchemist a unique point of view.

Think about Rube Goldberg and his thought process as he tried to make the most complicated machine to solve the simplest problem. He had to put his focus on systems, and not on the end product. Just think about Professor Butts and his napkin. The entire concept for the cartoon revolves around the system, the machine, the process for using the napkin, and not on the napkin itself. In fact, to get the point across, it doesn't matter what the napkin is made of. It could be cloth, paper, or sandpaper for all we know. What we do know about this cartoon, is that there is a system in place to deliver the napkin to the end customer. In this case, Professor Butts himself.

When referring to Rube Goldberg Curiosity, I'm not suggesting spending time making the most useless system you possibly could create. The Curiosity piece of developing Rube Goldberg Curiosity is the key to this exercise. Synaptic Alchemists in the Rubedo phase will become completely obsessed with the systems required to deliver their idea to the largest cohort of their audience.

It is this curiosity to explore systems, the curiosity to look at every nook and cranny of system design, the willingness to be curious about process and to release the end product, that will drive the alchemist at this stage.

There are many fantastic resources that explore systems thinking. Everything from W. Edwards Deming's Total Quality

Management to the processes of Six Sigma and its various manufacturing levels. There are manufacturing systems, quality control systems, software development lifecycles, you name it. What all of these have in common is that they are tactics and techniques used to implement systems.

As an alchemist you will need to transcend, to operate at a higher level than just the tactics and techniques. These tactics are all necessary and fantastic ways to implement a system. They are part of the How. How do I make the system efficient and cost-effective? As an alchemist your job is to contemplate the Why and What well before you worry about the How.

Intentions matter. Why does the system you are contemplating need to exist? Is it for speed of delivery? Is it for quality control? Then comes the What. What will the system produce? Standard products? Products and services that are easy to audit?

When building systems for my company, it became a challenge to integrate different systems for different purposes. The creative energies that were focused on ideation found a new home with system development. And yep, we made systems that were way too complicated for their intended purposes. But that's where the next section, on Ockham's razor, comes in.

OCKHAM'S RAZOR

Who is Ockham and why do we care about his razor? What does all this have to do with the alchemy of ideas and innovation? These are great questions and I'm glad you asked. It is a simple idea about … well … keeping things simple. The idea of Ockham's razor is attributed to an English Franciscan friar, William of Ockham (c 1287-1347)[58]. It is a simple problem-solving idea that all "entities should not be multiplied without necessity." There have been many other incarnations of the principle, the one I've heard most often is: "the simplest explanation is most likely the right one."

There are plenty of other ways to express Ockham's razor (which is also known as Occam's razor and Ocham's razor, and finally as the law of parsimony). KISS is one of the design principles used by the U.S. Navy back in 1960. The acronym stands for "Keep It Simple, Stupid" and it has been utilized in a variety of incarnations. The idea is to find the simplest solution that produces the intended output. Remember, intention matters. So, coming up with your intention when engaging in systems thinking is vital.

You may have heard of this in other ways, such as Leonardo da Vinci's "Simplicity is the ultimate sophistication." Or the quote from Antonine de Saint-Exupery, "Perfection is achieved, not when there is nothing more to add, but when there is nothing to left to take away." Or a paraphrase from Albert Einstein, "make everything as simple as possible, but not simpler."

This seems a direct contradiction to the anti-KISS point of view of Rube Goldberg, but they fit together. Because Rube Goldberg curiosity is all about falling in love with process and systems. It is the curiosity and not the complexity that we crave as alchemists. When you pair that with Ockham's razor or KISS you'll find that the curiosity will let you explore all the corners of systems while applying a "make it simpler" mindset.

This absolutely requires you to have an intention. Your intention becomes your guidepost. Your intention gives you something to measure against.

There is both art and science here. The art comes in defining your intention. At CID, we looked at what metrics a system would need to have that our customers would care about. Did we get it right every time and the first time out of the gate? Ha. Nope. Actually, we usually required many, many, many tries at fine tuning and simplifying our processes. There were so many late nights where I would ask myself: "What do my customers really want and what systems do we need to provide that?" And, many times, I would scream that into the void and wait for a response, but all I would hear was silence.

That's the point right there. The silence is a signal that you need to go back and watch and interact with and understand your customers. This time, not from an ideation point of view, but from a systems or delivery point of view. There were many, many times when we thought streamlining digital communications was of paramount importance to our customers. That would inspire us to build these complicated systems to support that. However, in reality, the systems that really mattered to our customers involved helping them take old school paper and securely, safely and quickly get that old paper into our digital systems. That is when we started to pour gold into our alchemical molds.

GET OPINIONATED

When was the last time someone told you that being opinionated was a good thing? It probably doesn't happen too often. Usually a statement like, "you're really opinionated," is really a polite way of saying "you're too damn opinionated and you think your opinion is THE only way of doing things."

I've heard this so many times in the past it is hard to count. It is part of my personality to be opinionated. Justifiably opinionated, hopefully, but opinionated nonetheless. What does it mean to be justifiably opinionated? I know I'm going to get a ton of pushback on that phrase. It means that your opinion is well thought through. It means that you have collected the data and analyzed the options and you have chosen a direction, and that direction best supports your intended plans. There is that word again. Intention. It matters. The Merriam-Webster dictionary defines intend as:

> "to have in mind as a purpose or goal"[59]

During this time—the get opinionated time—your intention matters most. This is because your opinion will express your intention directly. Let me show you what I mean. In running CID, we had to decide what we thought was the best way to both quickly get second medical opinions to our customers as well as maintain the highest quality in the industry. That was our intention: SPEED AND QUALITY. That AND in the middle is a key Synaptic Alchemist mindset. That AND concept is called "Avoiding the Tyranny of the Or, and Embracing the Beauty of the And." Although there is too much to explore on the Or-to-And mindset in this chapter, just the fact that we decided on that intention made all the difference.

Once we had our overarching intention at CID: SPEED AND QUALITY, we started getting opinionated. The intention was our North Star. A balancing act of a star for sure. But a North Star without a doubt. In our next step, since we knew our What, our North Star, we started thinking about the How. Not the detailed how of a Total Quality Management process or Six Sigma engagement. Rather the conceptual how. We asked the following question:

How are we going to deliver our intention?

Did we know we were asking ourselves that question? Well, sometimes. Sometimes we would be intentional, and sometimes it would just bubble up by happenstance. As the company matured, we became much more intentional about asking that question. The answer eventually made itself very clear. We needed to get the Right Doctors, the Right Information, at the Right Time. You'll notice that we didn't say "come up with the right answer," because that is something we couldn't measure. A high-quality analysis by the right experts in the shortest period of time was something we could deliver on and measure.

Great. Now we had our intention: Speed AND Quality. And we knew how to get there. The Right Doctors, The Right Information, at the Right Time. Now it was time for us to get opinionated.

That's exactly what we did. We built systems (remember we're in the Rubedo, i.e. systemization phase). Software systems. Recruiting systems. QA / QC systems. Oversight systems. Audit systems. We built systems like crazy. Some of them were automated. Some were manual. Some started manual and we automated little pieces. Some were manual but we made them more efficient as we understood them better. We mapped out processes (in fact we used a software tool called Simul8 and mapped out every single step in our company and inside our clients as well) and went to work making decisions about the best way to implement that process.

That's when we became opinionated. We spent the time and energy to figure out the best way to go from "The Right

Doctors, The Right Information, at the Right Time" to "Speed AND Quality" and that meant we made decisions on how things would work.

Those decisions weren't always popular, both internally and with our clients. Sometimes our clients wanted things just so. Just a little different. And we would have to say No. We would tell our customers and potential customers that we had already looked at things that way, and that was not the best way to accomplish our stated goals.

Oh, were they mad at times. Sometimes they would listen. Sometimes they would just walk away, and we would lose that client. Those times hurt. But we knew that to take our idea and pour that golden idea into golden molds, we would have to standardize. And to standardize means you have to take a position, have an opinion, and stay with that opinion. That's part of Geoffrey Moore's "Inside the Tornado" and it is part of the Rubedo phase of Synaptic Alchemy. Standardize and get opinionated.

FRICTION

You know it when you feel it. Friction is the resistance that one surface or object encounters when moving over another. We experience friction in the real world in the form of the amount of effort it takes to get something done. And friction is all over the place. It's not just when you put a piece of sandpaper on a piece of wood and you can really FEEL the friction. It exists in places that we don't necessarily know about, but it is there nonetheless.

Friction can be hidden in plain sight. Just think about a car. We all understand that there is friction between the tires and the road. That's the good kind of friction. That is the type that keeps our car on the road. If you have ever driven on an icy road and your car slips all over the place, you viscerally understand how much you miss that friction. As your car skids all over the road and you struggle to keep control, the connection between your car and the road is loosened to the point where you lose control. So that type of friction, the type

316

that keeps different things together that you want kept together, like a car and the road, or your employees and payroll, is a good thing.

We all know that friction can also be something to avoid. Think about that car again. Inside the car engine we know there are pistons that move up and down that eventually makes the car move. When you press on the gas pedal the parts of your engine start to move. But they are kind of stuck together. They do not necessarily move as silky smooth as you would like. They actually kind of stick and grind. That is why you use oil. You use oil to lubricate the parts of your car that you want to work smoothly. The better the oil, the lower the friction and the lower the wear and tear on your car and its parts. You also know what happens to that oil. It eventually gets dirty and without paying attention to it, without getting an oil change, that oil slowly loses its ability to keep things moving as freely as possible.

What does all this have to do with Synaptic Alchemy? How does all this talk about friction relate to Rubedo and systems thinking? It has everything to do with the conversion, the transformation, of an idea from just an idea into a real-life experience that we all can benefit from. The heat, the amount of effort it takes to grease the wheels of alchemy, is just another type of friction. Alchemists, especially modern-day Synaptic Alchemists, are masters of friction management. When it comes to identifying and reducing the amount of friction in your systems, whether those systems are part of delivering your product / service / idea or they are part of getting your audience's attention, friction management and reduction is crucial.

The idea of friction is something we are used to in the physical world, and that idea translates to the world of Alchemy, systematization and delivery extremely well. Ignoring friction when you are looking to scale the wisps of an idea into something tangible will get you in trouble. Ignoring friction will have you running full speed ahead into quicksand when you thought you were on solid ground, or getting stuck in stormy weather when you thought you had smooth sailing ahead of you.

So, how do you translate the idea of friction from the physical world to the world of Synaptic Alchemy and especially in the case of innovation? This is what we are doing in Rubedo. We are smoothing the way between the idea and the outside world. First, you will need to identify all of the potential connection points from your idea to the outside world. Then, you need to figure out the Coefficient of Friction at each of those touch points, i.e. how much heat and energy it takes to move over a specific part of friction, and what type of alchemical process you need to apply to reduce that heat. It might sound like part of that college Physics class you took early on (and it is), or it may seem like magic (it isn't). It is just a new way of looking at the layer between your idea and your audience.

Alchemists have been paying attention to and managing friction since they first attempted to transform lead into gold and from when they first started to think about transformation as a part of the natural process of creating valuable substances. Crossing the membrane between idea and audience is just friction management. Reduce this unwanted friction (the difficulty of interacting with or getting your hands on, or playing with, or operating, or maintaining something) impeding your alchemical idea, and the resulting improvement in your ability to implement your concept on the ground can be astonishing.

Friction itself can be thought of really as a cost of doing business, whether that business is a physical transformation or a conceptual one. Think of friction as a byproduct of entropy; which means that you can think of managing friction as reducing the entropy in a system.

The coefficient of friction is simply a measurement of how much friction there is in a system. Think of it like a thermometer. The more friction there is in a system, the harder it is for something to work, the higher the coefficient of friction. On a scale of 0-10 where 0 means there is no friction and 10 means things are really stuck, you want to consciously guide your ideas towards 0. Where does the membrane of friction exist? Where do you measure the coefficient of friction? Well it mostly (not always) exists at the membrane between your idea and your customer along each of the points of contact where your idea meets the outside world. That is why it is critical to know where your idea is rubbing against the outside world and to apply some alchemical magic at each of those spots.

TYPES OF FRICTION

Friction comes in many different flavors, shapes and sizes, as friction is created by the boundaries between systems. It is a natural extension of how two different things meet. When we think about friction in the real world, we usually think about one object on top of another and how much effort we have to devote to get one thing to move.

As you start to think about reducing friction across your business, you will find that there are many different types of frictions. Many different ways that slow the distribution of your idea down and make it harder or costlier to turn your inputs into real revenue.

IDENTIFICATION FRICTION

How quickly and easily your audience can find you, and then identify that by finding you they gain access to a solution to either a problem they were looking to solve or a unique idea that they can dive into, directly translates into Identification Friction.

Identification Friction = The amount of effort to find and identify your solution as valuable

The first part of identification friction is typically considered by economists to be search costs. The best example of a reducer of search costs or Identification Friction is Google. Google generates over $100B annually in ad revenue to help users more effectively solve the search component of Identification Friction (ad revenue for the four quarters ending Q2 '18 was reported from Alphabet, Google's parent company, as $106B).

How easy is it for your customers to find you outside of using Google? How many questions can users ask themselves that you might be able to answer? This is a different way of thinking. It requires you to put yourself in your potential customers' shoes and think about what questions they are internally asking themselves (not necessarily explicitly asking) that would lead them to search for you. The more questions that your product and service might answer, the more touch points you have. That increases your ability to interact with potential buyers and is a lubricant for searching.

The next piece of the puzzle to understanding Identification Friction is suitability. How likely is a customer to think you are uniquely qualified to solve their problem or to find what you offer interesting enough to pique their curiosity? This comes down to the ability of the customer to identify you as a way to fulfill their desires.

Suitability is not factual nor based on your capabilities. Suitability is based on your customers' perceptions. How well they FEEL you fit in with their plans. Whether those plans are to solve a problem or to discover something new. This again requires you to see the world through your customers' eyes. To understand their intentions better than they do.

Nike is a pure example of identification friction. We know that Nike is associated with sports, and specifically athletic footwear. The association of Nike's brand with some of the most iconic athletes[60] of our era, including: Michael Jordan, Tiger Woods, Bo Jackson, and many more, has reduced identification friction to almost zero. The core of brand building. Nike's rise to the top of their industry absolutely hinged on how customers feel Nike fits into their athletic plans, above and beyond the athletes the brand is linked to. That is

323

reflected in their "Just Do It" slogan, which makes their customers feel that they too can realize their athletic objectives.

Addressing identification friction leads us back to Harvard Business School Professor Clayton Christensen's jobs-to-be-done framework from "The Innovator's Solution". In the jobs-to-be-done framework, customers are looking for a tool to help them accomplish some objective (whether that is a physical objective or an emotional one). That objective may be a need to solve a problem or a way to experience a desire. The suitability component of Identification Friction is to reduce the amount of effort (emotionally, intellectually, etc.) that your customers must expend for them to feel that you or your idea IS the solution they are looking for.

How to reduce Identification Friction

You'll have to identify both components of Identification Friction to be able to understand how to make it easier for people who care about your idea to find and actually engage with you.

1) Record a listing of every question you can think of that someone may ask or have in their head about a problem you solve or a discovery they could engage with. This list is not exhaustive by any means and surely is not accurate as it comes from your point of view. But it is THE key to start you on the road towards addressing

search touch points. This starts to come full circle within the Alchemical Transformation as it touches upon the work you did in Albedo.

2) Write down each and every location that a user will use these questions or terms to find you. This could be a query on Google which eventually would become an AdWords search term or could be the title of an article on Medium. The goal here is to come up with a set of locations that a user will search. It is kind of like making a listing of where you would look if you lost your car keys. It is a search grid of sorts.

3) Now that you know where your audience is looking, you will need to start to understand how you can position your idea in these places. This is a tricky part and a part that requires you to determine costs and revenue and efficiency of attention. But now that you know where your audience is, you can start to position yourself there.

4) Congratulations, you have positioned yourself where your audience is looking. Now you have to reduce the friction with your audience, so they believe you are suitable to fulfill their desires. Reducing suitability friction requires you to understand what your audience has used in the past to accomplish their goals. This is

where the jobs-to-be-done framework comes into play. Write down a listing of the jobs you believe your audience is attempting to accomplish. This can flow from your search questions in the above step.

5) Now that you have a listing of jobs you believe your audience is attempting to fulfill, you will need to see what they have done in the past to get these jobs done. A straightforward local example could be a dentist. A dentist might not be fulfilling the job "Help me get rid of my tooth ache", but might be fulfilling many other jobs, such as "make my smile as bright as it can be". You now have an idea about a job that your audience believes you are suitable to fulfill. Write down each and every tool your customers have used to handle that job.

6) Crafting messages that specifically relate to that job is vital. Messages that directly identify how you are the most suitable resource IS key to reducing the suitability component of Identification Friction. Compiling a listing of the messaging will give you a starting point to for reducing this friction.

USAGE FRICTION

How frustrated did you get the last time you sat down to use something, and it was just hard to use? If you are like most people, crazy frustrated. Then, how many times have you said to yourself: "I won't buy this terrible thing again." Those are the types of emotions that get people to write horrible reviews on Yelp.

Go to a restaurant and see what it feels like when it is hard to get the waiter's attention, or they bring you the wrong item, or the item that you ordered is just not quite right. If you think about the experience that your customer has when using your product, how easy is it for them to actually do so? That is usage friction: How many clicks, what is the waiting time, how easy are the instructions, are all the right pieces in place?

This is what technology designers call "Ease of Use." But it's not just for technology. It is for ALL concepts, products, and services, no matter what you do. Everything—and I mean everything—your customer does with you is part of their usage. The harder it is to understand, or the longer it takes to accomplish, or the more steps it requires to get to the end, the higher the friction and the lower the chance you will get a repeat customer, much less a raving fan.

How to identify Usage Friction

This is a pretty straightforward process, however, identifying Usage Friction takes time, work, and a desire to really find out how good you and your product or service truly are.

1) Observe your customers in as many different situations as possible and create a listing of every interaction they have with your business. And I mean EVERY SINGLE INTERACTION. You cannot skip steps on this. If your customer buys a product on your web site, then gets the product delivered, then registers the product, you have at least three (and probably many more) touchpoints. Write them all down.

2) For each interaction, record how many touchpoints the customer had to engage with to accomplish the interaction. For example, if it takes 12 clicks on your website to order a product (this is after searching your website which is a different interaction) then you have 12 touchpoints for the Ordering interaction.

3) For each touchpoint, record the length of time it took for the customer to accomplish the touchpoint. If you are at a restaurant, figuring out what to order is one interaction. Having to look at the wine menu, and the dinner menu, and the chalkboard for today's specials is

three touchpoints. If it takes two minutes at each touchpoint record that time for each interaction.

You now have your coefficient of friction for your usage. Reduce this. Reduce the number of clicks. The number of steps. The number of touch points. The time to execute a touch point. You can increase your quality at the touchpoints that are absolutely crucial. But reduce the overall friction.

ADOPTION FRICTION

People don't change. That is an axiom that I firmly believe in. Well, they don't change without a substantial amount of pressure from many different sides. Change can occur when there is a new way of doing things that drastically, and I mean by 10x or more, reduces the hassle of doing something. That hassle may show up as financial cost or time spent or required emotional energy. Or change can occur when an emotional trigger gets pulled on hard enough and enough times. Think about the fear of missing out that causes someone to start to use social media. It is only when enough of their tribe is using a certain platform that they relinquish their traditional methods and try something new.

With all of that being said, change will only occur when there is a 10x difference or significant emotional force. I still stand by my original statement. People don't change. I'm not going to go into the reasoning behind why people don't change. Actually, there is a substantial amount of research on why people don't change their behaviors in any easy to affect or short-term fashion. Sometimes even when the circumstances are dire, such as losing your life, people still don't do what is necessary, as explained in the book *Change or Die*[61] .

The resistance people have to changing how they do something is the adoption friction facing an idea. The more behaviors I have to change, the more different steps I have to take, the newer concepts I have to understand, the lower my willingness to change will be and the higher the Adoption Friction.

How to identify Adoption Friction

This can be more elusive than it first seems. Again, the ability for you to see the world through your audience's eyes is paramount to understanding how much Adoption Friction your idea has to contend with. Putting in the effort needed to explore behavior patterns yields a better understanding of adoption friction.

1) Make a listing of the physical changes necessary for your audience to think about, operate, or engage with your idea. A complete list. For example, if a customer has to park and walk 1 block because you have moved to a new location, where they used to just be able to park and jump into your store in 10 feet, you have increased adoption friction. A listing of physical changes is the first step to understanding this type of friction.

2) Make a listing of new steps your audience will have to perform to engage with you. These new steps could be physical such as filling out a form and mailing something in, or digital such as going to a new web site

or clicking through to get an offer. A good example of this in reverse, where people wanted to increase adoption friction, is with rebate cards. Have you ever noticed how difficult it is to actually get your rebate? You have to fill out a form, remember to send in part of your purchase packaging, then you don't just get cash, you get a prepaid credit card with an expiration date. According to industry surveys, although 60 percent of all shoppers prefer products with rebates, only 10 percent of them actually redeem the offer. This is a clear use of adoption friction for a specific purpose.

3) Make a listing of the new thought processes your audience will need to engage with to adopt your idea. Is there new vocabulary they need to learn? Or do they need to really consume a new concept in detail? The more complicated it is to adopt your idea, the higher the adoption friction. Stephen Hawking, the world-renowned physicist, is quoted as saying "Someone told me that each equation I included in the book would halve the sales"[62] when speaking of his book 'A Brief History of Time'.[63] He was intelligent enough to only put in one equation: $E=MC^2$. A marker of adoption friction reduction in its truest sense.

You now know how much you need to simplify your idea in order to get people to adopt it. Take each of the lists you made above and cut, cut, cut. Simplify, simplify, simplify. Reduce the amount of friction people must experience to adopt your idea. Focus on creating huge decreases in hassle or a true reduction in emotional burdens.

CULTURAL FRICTION

How much do other people's opinions increase the discomfort of doing something? In California, the interactions, stares and looks of disdain you would get for smoking cigarettes indoors became so intense that, even before state laws banned the use of cigarettes in workplaces and certain public spaces, it became almost impossible to continue to use cigarettes without having to constantly defend your behavior.

In Copenhagen, 62% of the population bike to work every day and the vast majority keep it up through the cold and wet winter weather. But that's not just because it is the healthy choice, but because it is the easiest choice.[64] The city is designed for bikes and not cars. The infrastructure, which is a manifestation of the culture, has consciously increased the friction for using cars.

Going against cultural friction and attempting to manifest an idea that clearly does not use cultural friction to its advantage is surely an expensive exercise. Building a new car or car parts store or car wash in Copenhagen will not get you very far, as that specifically increases cultural friction.

Although cigarettes have had a rough time in culturally sensitive yet lucrative areas of the United States, vaping has capitalized on that friction by offering a culturally acceptable alternative. Until now, that is. Recently, article after article (for example, a headline in a Heart Association article about vaping states: "Many downsides. Few potential upsides")[65] has promoted the idea that vaping is potentially just as dangerous if not more so than cigarettes, and the expected increase in cultural friction has materialized.

Understanding how the culture perceives your idea can be elusive since there is not just one culture. There are many cultures:

Societal: The culture of society at large. This could be a national, state, regional or local cultural norm. For example, some East Coast regions have a highly intense culture of political activism. Understanding the society in which you operate or are attempting to deploy your idea and the intensity of the friction of that culture is imperative.

Workplace / Organizational: Companies, schools, professional organizations all have their own cultural norms, and all have put in place either institutional or accepted behavioral standards which will affect cultural friction.

Familial / Personal: Families, groups of friends, cliques, they all have their cultural norms and corresponding cultural friction. Have a clear understanding that these norms exist and how much friction is associated with each of them.

How to identify Adoption Friction

You'll need to go from the largest group, or group that has the most ability to enforce their culture either through infrastructure or through behavior, to the smallest. But don't skimp. A small cultural friction can cause a large problem if it comes out of the blue. Cultural frictions can be managed or adhered to, but you'll need to figure out which ones affect your idea.

1) Start with the most enforceable cultural norm. This typically will be the one with the largest number of members, but that is not always necessarily true. Write down the cohort that owns the norm (e.g. the Teacher's Union) and write down the norm that they adhere to.

2) Once you have a listing of the cultural touch points you will need to understand what the friction is related to. Is the friction supported by infrastructure (e.g. not easy for cars to drive in Copenhagen)? Or is it supported by cultural opinion?

3) Now that you have a listing and understand the cultural touch points, you'll need to come up with a plan to address each and every one. You won't get your coefficient of friction down to zero. There will always be some friction in the system. But having a plan to

reduce the friction at heavy touch points IS the key to having a manageable coefficient of cultural friction.

Now that you know how many cultural friction touchpoints you need to address, you have an idea of the coefficient of friction for the cultural environment you are operating in. Knowing this in advance and preparing a plan for managing these touch points is absolutely essential to the adoption of your concept.

GOVERNMENTAL FRICTION

You may think that if you are not in a regulated industry that understanding governmental friction is not part of your world. Sometimes you may be right. However, there are many components of the government that you may think you don't have to deal with, while in reality doing so is very much a significant part of turning your idea from lead into gold.

The first, most impactful and obvious connection to governmental friction is if you live and breathe in a regulated industry such as healthcare. But before you start saying: "I'm not in a regulated industry," you should double check whether your customers are in a regulated industry. Regulation is not just about your specific world, but about the worlds with which you interact. If your customer is in a regulated industry, then you are too, even if only tangentially.

Let me give you a real-life example. In my last company, we provided service and software to insurance companies and administrators who managed patient treatment decisions. To be clear, my company was not responsible for approving or deciding which treatments were being given. We either sold software to provide information or had physicians who provided second opinions. At no point did our team even get close to delivering treatment or treatment decisions. However, our customers did. Since our customers had to comply with all local, state and federal laws, so did we. We took measures to become HIPAA compliant, otherwise our customers would not do business with us. If someone in our ecosystem was required to follow governmental laws, best practices, or standards then so did we. If not, our customers wouldn't be our customers for very long.

As you look into governmental friction, pay attention not only to the required steps you need to take to transform your idea into an executing mission, but also pay attention to the governmental requirements for everyone in your ecosystem. And I mean everyone. That includes suppliers, vendors, labor markets, customers, and distribution channels.

Think about markets that have partial legal exposure, such as cannabis. As it stands in early 2019, recreational marijuana is legal in 10 states across the U.S. and medical marijuana is legal in 33 states. However, it is still illegal federally. This creates some interesting governmental friction. Not just friction across the legality of operating in the cannabis market, but governmental friction at the tax level (look at section 280e of the IRS code) as well as where you are in the supply chain (e.g. if you write software specifically for dispensaries are you considered part of the cannabis supply chain?).

How to identify Governmental Friction

Since friction between you and the government can arise at many different points, from federal regulations and tax laws to state and local fees, technical requirements, regulatory filings, best practices and not just of your business but of your entire ecosystem, you will need to do a deep dive to ensure you are complying. Being out of compliance with governmental requirements can be very expensive to remedy.

1) Write a list of your ecosystem. Who will you need to work with your idea? If you need employees, how will you hire them? Will they be local or across state lines, within the US or abroad, physically located at offices or virtual? Look at your supply chain, do they have requirements imposed on them from the government (e.g. required filing types such as electronic with a short window). Look at your customers to see if they have compliance issues. This mapping of the ecosystem in which your ideas live and are birthed gives you a good outline as to where you sit within the world and where you rub up against governmental boundaries.

2) Make a list of each regulation (start from the largest, i.e. federal, and trickle down to the local) that each one of the constituents in your ecosystem must adhere too. Then add to these regulations any best practices,

340

certifications, or data requirements you need to adhere to the requirements.

3) Start a brainstorming session to determine potential ways to adhere to the regulations. Sometimes complying means implementing technology. Sometimes it requires certification. Sometimes it means getting approval by agencies. Sometimes it will change the way you setup your idea.

You now have a map of your governmental friction points. Being able to view this map in advance of encountering the friction gives you a head start. Sometimes understanding and adhering to regulations or best practices will give you an advantage. And sometimes it is just the cost of being an alchemist.

Rubedo All Wrapped Up

Rubedo is where we are breathing life into our alchemical creation. It is where we pour the gold we have smelted into molds and create the castings that the world will see. Rubedo is all about the creation of systems to produce and disseminate our alchemical ideas to the world. It is about changing our focus from a single point of view of ideation and discovery and moving that point of view to the systems required to nurture our idea.

There is a lot of art in each phase of Synaptic Alchemy, but the change in perspective in Rubedo makes it even more of a jarring transition. That is a key distinction of Rubedo from the other alchemical phases. Idea -> System. Once you have crossed that mindset juncture then getting the tools under your fingers is the easy part. That's how all of the phases of the alchemical transformation work. The mindset, the paradigm shift, the change in point of view away from what may be your natural tendency is where all the work and all the value is created. Being able to cross into this last phase is what will create real wealth, birth true transformation, and let the world see and experience the golden creation you have so carefully developed.

Now that you have gone from disintermediation to creation to scale, it is time for you to start building up your toolkit and collecting the specialized tools you will need to continue to grow as an alchemist.

6. THE ALCHEMICAL TOOLKIT

$1,001

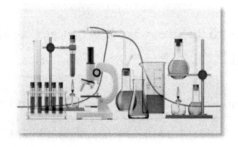

A while ago I was introduced to an older, proper gentleman. His demeanor led me to believe that although he did not graduate from an Ivy League university, nor did he ever climb to the top of the corporate ladder, he had a grace and wisdom about him that was unusually clear. I asked him about his profession. He told me that he was retired and that he had been in the heating and air conditioning business. But he just couldn't seem to retire.

He was constantly getting calls from various companies to help out with their latest installation or help fix a problem here or a malfunction there. That seemed like a very gentle retirement, so I asked him about the last time he went out on a job.

"Well, about a month ago, the CEO of my old company called me up and said: 'We're trying to install this giant system on the top floor of this 35-story building and it just isn't working. Can you please help?' I didn't really want to, but I figured I'd help out my old boss," he said.

Even though the story was pretty typical, I couldn't help but be transfixed.

He continued: "So I got to the address and went to the building. There it was, a big 35-story glass tower. I told security that I was there to fix the A/C. We jumped in the elevator and they took me up to the top floor where all the equipment was housed."

"It was huge. I don't know, maybe 20,000 square feet of equipment. I didn't know where to look. But my intuition was tingling. There was something in the back corner that didn't seem right. Maybe I caught sight of a wire loose or out of place when I was surveying the floor. I didn't quite know. But I went over, balled my hand up into a fist and slammed it into the machinery."

"The entire floor started to whirl and suddenly the A/C was working. I walked back past the stunned security guard and we headed down."

"I got home and sent the CEO my bill. That's when I got the call. My old boss called me and asked why he was getting billed for $1,001? I said 'well, $1 is for hitting your air conditioning system. The other $1,000 is for knowing where.'"

I love that parable. I don't remember where I first heard it. I know it's not true and I can feel the "not true" part early on in the story. But the idea, the parable, of having your bag of $1,001 tools fits so perfectly.

Why should you care about $1,001 tools and why other people will want them? Well, there are a couple of reasons:

1. You only pay the learning costs for your $1,001 skill once. The first time you learn it. That is the most expensive moment. After that, every time you use your $1,001 skill, you essentially reduce the overall skill / use cost. Just think, once you've used your skill 1,001 times, if you incurred a $1,001 learning cost, then you are down to a $1 / use cost—a pretty good use of your time.

2. Maybe other people could learn what you know. But then they'd have to pay the leaning cost first. That most expensive moment. And unless they plan on using that same skill and re-selling it to others, then you are the much cheaper, faster, and more experienced alternative. For example, if you charge $10 / use for your skill, but you are only incurring $1 / use in terms of cost, then your $1,001 skill is incredibly valuable, both for you and for your customer.

This is one of the things that Synaptic Alchemists do, they accumulate $1,001 tools. When you start to use the same thinking and apply it to processes and mindsets, your value as an alchemist grows exponentially.

Start collecting your $1,001 skills. Start building your $1,001 alchemical toolkit. Not only will you benefit but so will your audience. With that in mind, let's start exploring some tools.

Fail, Forward, Fast

"Why would anyone want to fail on purpose?" That was the question that was posed to me when I first said those words. Actually, I think I said the following:

"I want you to figure out how to fail as quickly as possible. Make strategic goofs. I mean, if you knew the right answer you would already be doing it, right? I'm not talking about 'bet the farm' kind of failures. I'm talking about goofing up with a plan, with an intention."

Most of my team looked at me with sideways glances, as if I had lost my mind.

This fits with another one of the alchemical mindsets: "Ask for forgiveness not permission."

We all make mistakes. We all have ideas and attempt things that don't work out as planned. That's the interesting thing. We call them failures or mistakes when the outcome doesn't match our preconceived notions, our expectations. So, what if we changed our expectations from "always being right in advance" to "experimenting with ideas."

What alchemists are in search of is mistakes, not complete failures. Mistakes = learning. Mistakes = Strategic goofs. Mistakes = Motion.

That fits with another alchemical mindset: "Don't get attached to outcome."

This trio of alchemical mindsets 1.) Fail, Forward, Fast 2.) Ask forgiveness not permission and 3.) Don't get attached to outcome, help you create a unique mindset that very few not only know about, but can really integrate into their daily routine.

We are taught in school that we're supposed to have the right answer to all the questions posed by the teachers. But that is not how life works, and that most definitely is not how alchemy works. We don't have the answers. The problems are not deterministic. Most of life is decision making under uncertainty.

Since we know that turning ideas into gold will require experimentation and a loose grasp on future circumstances rather than an iron first to control our environment, I highly recommend the Fail, Forward, Fast approach.

What are the elements of a Fail, Forward, Fast strategy?

Fail: When the outcome does not match the expected result, we believe we have failed. Then failing is exactly that, missing an expected or projected outcome. That is what alchemists do on a consistent basis. We make guesses as to what an outcome will be, and then design experiments to see what actually happens.

It is this commitment to experimentation that is a hallmark of alchemy. Not only a willingness to be wrong, and then to change course with new information, but a drive to make mistakes ... to fail. All organizations, groups, teams, and individuals who subscribe to the paradigm of "wanting a mistake" will—in the final analysis—wind up much further ahead than those who believe, with no evidentiary support, that their decisions are right in the first place.

So, here is the formula: 1.) Don't assume you know the outcome 2.) Create small experiments that have a clear-cut outcome 3.) Measure those experimental results 4.) Don't attempt to be right, attempt to learn.

Forward: This is a natural extension of the last item: "attempt to learn." That is what moving forward is all about. It is not about proving you were right in the first place. It is about generating knowledge so that your field of awareness and understanding expands. That is what it means to move forward. To have gained insights that you didn't have before.

These insights might be all about how an audience uses your product. Or they might be about how your idea is recognized throughout a community. It might be insights about your idea or your product, or insights about an audience or a community. Whatever insights they are, moving forward implies having more knowledge now than you did before.

Fast: Why do we need to do everything so damn quickly nowadays? That's a good question, with a racing car metaphor for an answer. Speed or cycle time is vitally important to increase your knowledge base as well as to stay relevant. In Formula One racing there is the 107% rule.[66] That rule means that as long as the roads are dry, you have to set a lap within 107% of the fastest time in the first qualifying season. So, if the fastest Q1 lap time was 60 seconds, you have to complete at least one lap within 64.2 seconds. This ensures that only the top drivers are included in the race.

Knowing that each time you make a mistake (remember making mistakes is different than failing) you are increasing your knowledge base, means that the more mistakes you make, the smarter you become. Becoming smart quickly matters in Synaptic Alchemy. Because the smarter you become, the closer you are to igniting the elixir that will turn your lead into gold.

AMAZON: THE BEST PLACE IN THE WORLD TO FAIL

In his 2016 shareholder letter, Amazon CEO Jeff Bezos famously stated that Amazon was "the best place in the world to fail."[67] Bezos intuitively understands that failure is not fatal. Failure means you are running experiments. His quote specifically underscores the alchemist mentality:

> "Failure and invention are inseparable twins. To invent you have to experiment, and if you know in advance that it's going to work, it's not an experiment."
>
> —Jeff Bezos, annual shareholder letter 2016

Amazon has had many experiments in their corporate history. Here are a few of the experiments that didn't work out as planned.[68]

1.) Fire phone - Amazon entered the incredibly competitive smartphone market in July 2014. The fierce competition from Apple's iPhone and Android phones proved more than considerable. Even an attempt to sell the phone for $0.99 did not work (which proves that pricing is not everything). Eventually Amazon wrote off a $170 million loss from the Fire phone project.

2.) Amazon wallet - A competitor to Apple Pay or Google Pay, the Amazon wallet only lasted for six months back in 2015. Designed as a way to store gift cards and loyalty cards, the lack of credit or debit cards and the massive competition from Apple and Google eventually proved too much for the digital wallet.

3.) Amazon WebPay - A competitor to PayPal and Venmo, the WebPay product was designed to allow direct consumer-to-consumer financial transactions. Started back in 2007, the product was discontinued in 2014 as the number of competitive products increased.

Amazon has made some strategic goofs. The point is … who cares? These are small goofs compared to Amazon Web Services (AWS), Marketplace, and Prime, any three of which could easily cover the losses. AWS itself generated $35 billion in sales in 2019. AWS was created back in 2000 as part of standardizing an Amazon offering called Merchant.com. That drive to create a smooth Merchant.com from the sea of services Amazon was already using for its own products is what created AWS.

Fail, Forward, Fast is the mantra of all successful companies, whether they are consciously aware of it (as in Amazon's case) or not, and a clear advantage of the alchemist approach.

How Do We Die Today?

Oooooh did my team hate it when I talked like this. The executive team, the sales team, even the operations team, wanted to be optimistic. They all wanted to see our ideas and our concepts play out in the real world. So did I. Actually, I am not a pessimistic person. I'm actually quite optimistic. In reality, you would call me … well … a realist. I have a desperate desire to have things turn out right. I'm also pretty competitive, so doing well is important to me. I'm mostly competitive with myself and want to be the best next version of myself each chance I get.

The realist part pertains in that I know there is so much I don't know. I don't really put much faith in hoping that things will work out in the way I want them to work out. So, I have a big picture vision which is optimistic, but my daily steps, the next steps—which is all I can control—are designed to be realistic. To be realistic means I am constantly looking for how things can go wrong. I am constantly looking for the landmines that I don't see that could blow up in my face. I am constantly on the lookout for things that might be fatal to the idea, the audience adoption, or the systems that are being built.

I don't know if Benjamin Franklin actually said the following (I'm paraphrasing), but it fits the alchemical philosophy:

"I'm an 'optimistic pessimist', I prepare for the worst, but when the very worst doesn't happen, I'm pleasantly surprised."

When you are using the "How Do We Die Today" alchemical mindset, all you are really asking is to do some intentional problem solving. Actually, you are looking to pre-solve potential problems before they come up. Some of the areas that you will need to explore are:

- Audience awareness: How can our audience not find us?

- Audience relevance: What can we do so that we are relevant to our audience?

- Audience usability: What steps will stop our customers from using our products?

- Audience acceptance: Why will our customers not accept or adopt our idea or products?

- Legal: What legal hurdles are we not paying attention to? Do we have our legal ducks all in a row? What about copyrights or trademarks? What about licensing?

- Operations: What will stop us from delivering our product, idea, solution at scale?

- Distribution: Think about the ways that your idea just can't get to your audience (e.g. if you are distributing a physical item internationally, have you thought through customs processing?).

I've stepped on many metaphorical landmines in my time. I've gotten better at detecting them in advance by asking the simple question: "How do we die today?" But, even so, I've stepped on my fair share.

One of the biggest blowups that hit me was Audience Acceptance. We developed a Software as a Service product for our audience. It truly was a well-crafted piece of software that automated many of the tasks of the employees of our corporate customers. And that was the landmine that set off the big boom.

It may not sound like a big boom from where you are sitting, and it didn't from where I was sitting when we were crafting the software, but it was … BOOM … our audience had a real resistance to our product.

Why? I asked that question myself. It automated a ton of work. The executives were very excited to see reduced costs AND increased quality. But the executives at our corporate customers were not our only audience. The people using the software were a whole other cohort. And you know what our software did for them? It made big chunks of their workflow irrelevant.

BOOM. That audience cohort found everything they could that was not perfect with our system. I didn't pay enough attention to that cohort, and we got some sales, but not enough. The people using our software didn't want to make their workflow irrelevant, and I stepped on that landmine much too late in the product offering.

Don't get me wrong. The software was a success where it was implemented. But we didn't get nearly as much customer adoption as I had predicted.

Lesson learned. The landmines are real and hidden. So, don't ignore them.

Your Alchemical Toolkit

"Use the Right Tool

For the Right Job

In the Right Way"

I don't know when I heard that for the first time. I don't know who is credited with coming up with that phrase nor when those words were first spoken. However, I do know that truer words were never spoken.

As a business person, a thought leader, a politician, a scientist, an entrepreneur, a lawyer, a doctor, or any professional, having the right tools is the difference between being able to deliver a quality product or service and just barely squeaking by, or not being able to deliver at all.

Tools give you the ability to quickly and, with high quality, handcraft solutions that exactly fit your needs. That is what the Synaptic Alchemy toolkit is all about. Not physical tools. Not emotional tools. But tools of the mind. Tools to impart vision. Tools that will make a difference with regard to what you see as important in your field of view, how you understand and perceive the external world, and how you create opportunities around situations that are difficult to understand.

That is why you need tools.

In fact, as CEO of my last company, we created 35 sound bites. 35 Commander's Intents (CI's) that described how the company ran. I learned about Commander's Intents from the book "Made to Stick: Why Some Ideas Survive and Others Die" by Chip and Dan Heath.[69] Their description of a "Commander's Intent",[70] which is an idea that guides without having to be specific, comes from the military in the 1980s. The Commander's Intent concept gave me explicit permission to create a toolkit for the company and the teams when they were in the field every day.

Our 35 sound bites, Commander's Intents, were the mindset tools that provided us with the vision and direction we needed as we encountered all sorts of twists and turns in building our business.

As you become a Synaptic Alchemist, creating your own personal toolkit constitutes a huge competitive advantage when it comes to your ability to engage your mind, lead your team and win the day by turning your ideas into gold.

7. THE ALCHEMIST'S JOURNEY

You have walked the path of the Synaptic Alchemist and made it to the end of this journey. Not the end of all journeys, but you've completed this one. That is cause for celebration; for taking a moment to breathe in the air of completion and be satiated with your success.

You have been exposed to many, many, many (and I do mean many) new ideas. Let them wash over you. Let them sink in. You are learning to think in ways that not many even attempt. This is how journeys change you. You see with new eyes.

"The real voyage of discovery consists, not in seeking new landscapes, but in having new eyes."

— Marcel Proust

That is where all the alchemical magic lies. In your eyes. In discovering a new way of interacting with the world and clearly seeing a new way to turn the ethereal matter of your thoughts into brilliant glowing golden riches, whether those riches are physical or not.

In this day and age, we are surrounded by alchemists. Some of them are household names like Elon Musk, Steven Spielberg, Lin-Manuel Miranda (the creator of Hamilton), Barack Obama, Stephen Hawking, Jeff Bezos (founder of Amazon), Larry Page and Sergey Brin (the founders and inventors of Google), and Bill Gates. Some of them, like Jennifer Doudna,[71] the co-founder of CRISPR which is a technology that can literally shape DNA, are names that you may not have on the tip of your tongue, but are nonetheless spectacular Synaptic Alchemists.

As a Synaptic Alchemist, you may be confronted with common wisdom that you'll have to shake off. You may be confronted with naysayers and critics. But none of that matters. Only the ability to turn ideas into gold matters. Only performance matters. The critics don't count. If you haven't heard of or read "The Man in the Arena" excerpt from President Theodore Roosevelt, the 26th President of the United States, now is a good time to let its wisdom wash over you.

"It is not the critic who counts; not the man who points out how the strong man stumbles, or where the doer of deeds could have done them better. The credit belongs to the man who is actually in the arena, whose face is marred by dust and sweat and blood; who strives valiantly; who errs, who comes short again and again, because there is no effort without error and shortcoming; but who does actually strive to do the deeds; who knows great enthusiasms, the great devotions; who spends himself in a worthy cause; who at the best knows in the end the triumph of high achievement, and who at the worst, if he fails, at least fails while daring greatly, so that his place shall never be with those cold and timid souls who neither know victory nor defeat."

—Theodore Roosevelt, April 23, 1910

You are now bound by an alchemical oath to think differently, to ignore the critics, and to create something beautiful and valuable from the tenuous wisps of thought that swirl around in your mind. That's what alchemists do. That is what Synaptic Alchemists must do, can't stop doing, and will always endeavor to do.

Don't think that the alchemical framework only relates to business or products or services. If your Synaptic mind comes up with an alchemical idea around your spouse or children, then cast that gold. If your Synaptic mind comes up with an alchemical idea to support your community or handcraft a public policy, then spin the threads of gold necessary to change your corner of the world.

Becoming a Synaptic Alchemist is a gift. It is a responsibility. It is a worthy challenge to take on in your life without ever looking back.

I invite you to join me on the quest of the Synaptic Alchemist. Bring your Philosopher's Stone as a magician, outlaw, jester, or whatever your stone reflects, ignite your Prima Materia and, for the rest of your days, turn ideas into gold.

ABOUT THE AUTHOR

Steven Cardinale is an entrepreneur and executive with 20+ years of business and technology experience. Mr. Cardinale brings his creative energies to exploring and understanding tactical strategies with time tested frameworks to recognize the common factors of successful ideas.

Through a unique perspective on leadership, innovation, startups, entrepreneurs and business strategy, Mr. Cardinale combines skills from experience as the founder and CEO of a successful Software as a Services company with the academic underpinnings acquired by receiving his MBA from The Wharton School of Business.

The combination of real-life experience, years of professional exploration, and academics from a top Ivy League university has given Mr. Cardinale a unique view for an in-depth exploration of the foundations of success.

NOTES

Acknowledgments

[1] "NYU Stern - Scott Galloway - Professor of Marketing," accessed July 27, 2020, https://www.stern.nyu.edu/faculty/bio/scott-galloway.

1. What's This All About

[2] "Elon Musk," Biography, accessed August 7, 2020, https://www.biography.com/business-figure/elon-musk.

[3] "Lin-Manuel Miranda," in *Wikipedia*, August 3, 2020, https://en.wikipedia.org/w/index.php?title=Lin-Manuel_Miranda&oldid=970920326.

[4] Michael Paulson and David Gelles, "'Hamilton' Inc.: The Path to a Billion-Dollar Broadway Show," *The New York Times*, June 8, 2016, sec. Theater, https://www.nytimes.com/2016/06/12/theater/hamilton-inc-the-path-to-a-billion-dollar-show.html.

[5] "Think Different," in *Wikipedia*, July 27, 2020, https://en.wikipedia.org/w/index.php?title=Think_different&oldid=969865617.

[6] "Individuation," in *Wikipedia*, August 10, 2020, https://en.wikipedia.org/w/index.php?title=Individuation&oldid=972229460.

[7] Carmine Gallo, "The Best Speech In The 'Game Of Thrones' Finale And Why It Matters To Today's leaders," Forbes, accessed July 26, 2020, https://www.forbes.com/sites/carminegallo/2019/05/22/the-best-speech-in-the-game-of-thrones-finale-and-why-it-matters-to-todays-leaders/.

[8] "Theatre of Dionysos Eleuthereus," Ancient History Encyclopedia, accessed July 26, 2020, https://www.ancient.eu/article/814/theatre-of-dionysos-eleuthereus/.

[9] Chip Heath and Dan Heath, *Made to Stick: Why Some Ideas Survive and Others Die*, 1st edition (New York: Random House, 2007).

[10] "Scale of the Human Brain," AI Impacts, April 16, 2015, https://aiimpacts.org/scale-of-the-human-brain/.

[11] David Goggins, *Can't Hurt Me: Master Your Mind and Defy the Odds* (Miejsce nieznane: Lioncrest Publishing, 2018).

[12] "How Edison Invented the Light Bulb — And Lots of Myths About Himself," Time, accessed September 19, 2020, https://time.com/3517011/thomas-edison/.

[13] Christensen, Clayton M., Jeff Dyer, and Hal Gregersen. The Innovator's DNA: Mastering the Five Skills of Disruptive Innovators. 1 edition. Harvard Business Review Press, 2011. Kindle edition. Location 517 of 3942

2. Why Synaptic Alchemy

[14] "Did Wayne Gretzky Coin the Phrase 'Skate to Where the Puck Is Going, Not to Where It Is'?," *Sports Urban Legends Revealed!* (blog), June 23, 2013,

http://legendsrevealed.com/sports/2013/06/22/did-wayne-gretzky-coin-the-phrase-skate-to-where-the-puck-is-going-not-to-where-it-is/.

[15] "How Alchemy Paved the Way for Chemistry | HowStuffWorks," accessed August 29, 2020, https://science.howstuffworks.com/alchemy-to-chemistry.htm; "How Alchemy Became Modern Chemistry," *BioFuelNet* (blog), May 28, 2015,

http://www.biofuelnet.ca/nce/2015/05/28/alchemy-tradition-spanning-millennia-became-modern-chemistry/.

[16] "Boyle's Law," in *Wikipedia*, August 20, 2020, https://en.wikipedia.org/w/index.php?title=Boyle%27s_law&oldid=974028642.

3. Personal Alchemical Exploration

[17] Chip Conley and Tony Hsieh, *PEAK: How Great Companies Get Their Mojo from Maslow Revised and Updated*, n.d.

[18] Rick Foster and Greg Hicks, *How We Choose to Be Happy: The 9 Choices of Extremely Happy People--Their Secrets, Their Stories*, n.d.

[19] "Flow (Psychology)," in *Wikipedia*, August 23, 2020, https://en.wikipedia.org/w/index.php?title=Flow_(psychology)&oldid=974458591.

[20] "Flow: The Psychology of Optimal Experience (Harper Perennial Modern Classics): Mihaly Csikszentmihalyi: 8601405917720: Amazon.Com: Books," accessed August 29, 2020, https://www.amazon.com/Flow-Psychology-Experience-Perennial-Classics/dp/0061339202.

4. The Philosopher's Stone

[21] "Coat of Arms | Definition, History, Symbols, & Facts," Encyclopedia Britannica, accessed September 30, 2020, https://www.britannica.com/topic/coat-of-arms.

[22] "Elon Musk's Mission to Mars | WIRED." Accessed February 29, 2020. https://www.wired.com/2012/10/ff-elon-musk-qa/.

5. The Alchemical Transformation

[23] Christensen, Clayton M., Taddy Hall, Karen Dillon, and David S. Duncan. "Know Your Customers' 'Jobs to Be Done.'" *Harvard Business Review*, September 1, 2016. https://hbr.org/2016/09/know-your-customers-jobs-to-be-done.

[24] HBS Working Knowledge. "What Customers Want from Your Products," January 16, 2006. http://hbswk.hbs.edu/item/what-customers-want-from-your-products.

[25] November 16 and 2012, "Mystery of Memory." https://www.livescience.com/24836-mystery-memory-recall.html

[26] Grothaus, Michael, and Michael Grothaus. "A Rediscovered 1997 Video Reveals Why Jeff Bezos Chose Books and Not CDs to Be Amazon's First Product." Fast Company, November 13, 2019. https://www.fastcompany.com/90430303/a-rediscovered-1997-video-reveals-why-jeff-bezos-chose-books-and-not-cds-to-be-amazons-first-product.

[27] "History of Yahoo!," in *Wikipedia*, August 27, 2020, https://en.wikipedia.org/w/index.php?title=History_of_Yahoo!&oldid=975332686.

[28] "How We Started and Where We Are Today - Google," accessed September 5, 2020, //www.google.com/our-story/.

29 "Negativity Bias." In Wikipedia, May 28, 2020. https://en.wikipedia.org/w/index.php?title=Negativity_bias&oldid=959467862.

30 Voss, Chris, and Tahl Raz. Never Split the Difference: Negotiating As If Your Life Depended On It. 1 edition. New York: Harper Business, 2016.

31 "Meisner Technique." In Wikipedia, May 21, 2020.
https://en.wikipedia.org/w/index.php?title=Meisner_techniq
ue&oldid=957971526.

32 "Big Three (Management Consultancies)." In Wikipedia,
July 10, 2020.
https://en.wikipedia.org/w/index.php?title=Big_Three_(man
agement_consultancies)&oldid=966941186.

33 Friga, Paul. The McKinsey Engagement: A Powerful
Toolkit For More Efficient and Effective Team Problem
Solving. 1 edition. New York: McGraw-Hill Education, 2008.

34 "It's a Wonderful Life." In Wikipedia, July 23, 2020.
https://en.wikipedia.org/w/index.php?title=It%27s_a_Wond
erful_Life&oldid=969126631.

35 "Sliding Doors." In Wikipedia, July 21, 2020.
https://en.wikipedia.org/w/index.php?title=Sliding_Doors&
oldid=968833885.

36 "The Matrix." In Wikipedia, July 20, 2020.
https://en.wikipedia.org/w/index.php?title=The_Matrix&old
id=968648862.

37 Psychologies. "George-Bailey-Effect." Text. Accessed July
26, 2020. https://www.psychologies.co.uk/george-bailey-
effect.

38 Koo, Minkyung, Sara B. Algoe, Timothy D. Wilson, and
Daniel T. Gilbert. "It's a Wonderful Life: Mentally Subtracting
Positive Events Improves People's Affective States, Contrary
to Their Affective Forecasts." Journal of Personality and
Social Psychology 95, no. 5 (November 2008): 1217–24.
https://doi.org/10.1037/a0013316.

39 Franklin-Wallis, Oliver. "Inside X, Google's Top-Secret
Moonshot Factory." Wired UK, February 17, 2020.
https://www.wired.co.uk/article/ten-years-of-google-x.

40 Psychology Today. "How Many Decisions Do We Make Each Day?" Accessed June 29, 2020. https://www.psychologytoday.com/blog/stretching-theory/201809/how-many-decisions-do-we-make-each-day.

41 "Shoshin." In Wikipedia, May 20, 2020. https://en.wikipedia.org/w/index.php?title=Shoshin&oldid=957849035.

42 Cerulli Associates. "Transfer of Wealth." Accessed July 13, 2020. https://info.cerulli.com/HNW-Transfer-of-Wealth-Cerulli.html.

43 InvestmentNews. "Robo-Advisers Continue Swift Asset Growth," February 3, 2020. https://www.investmentnews.com/robo-adviser-asset-growth-187680.

44 StatCounter Global Stats. "Search Engine Market Share Worldwide." Accessed July 14, 2020. https://gs.statcounter.com/search-engine-market-share.

45 Kim, Eugene. "Jeff Bezos: 'We Are the Best Place in the World to Fail.'" Business Insider. Accessed July 15, 2020. https://www.businessinsider.com/amazon-ceo-jeff-bezos-best-place-in-the-world-to-fail-2016-4.

46 "A Tech Reality: If You Don't like Change, You're Going to like Irrelevance Even Less | PhocusWire." Accessed July 16, 2020. https://www.phocuswire.com/A-tech-reality--If-you-don-t-like-change-you-re-going-to-like-irrelevance-even-less.

47 Emmer, Marc. "95 Percent of New Products Fail. Here Are 6 Steps to Make Sure Yours Don't." Inc.com, July 6, 2018. https://www.inc.com/marc-emmer/95-percent-of-new-products-fail-here-are-6-steps-to-make-sure-yours-dont.html.

48 "To the Nines." In Wikipedia, May 28, 2020.
https://en.wikipedia.org/w/index.php?title=To_the_nines&o
ldid=959287077.

49 "Top Hat, White Tie and Tails." In Wikipedia, May 21,
2020.
https://en.wikipedia.org/w/index.php?title=Top_Hat,_White
_Tie_and_Tails&oldid=958078943.

50 "Signalling (Economics)." In Wikipedia, June 3, 2020.
https://en.wikipedia.org/w/index.php?title=Signalling_(econ
omics)&oldid=960474735.

51 "Signalling Theory." In Wikipedia, June 26, 2020.
https://en.wikipedia.org/w/index.php?title=Signalling_theory
&oldid=964645760.

52 Writing Explained. "What Does All Dressed Up and
Nowhere to Go Mean?" Accessed July 16, 2020.
https://writingexplained.org/idiom-dictionary/all-dressed-up-
nowhere-to-go.

53 Gladwell, Malcolm. The Tipping Point: How Little Things
Can Make a Big Difference. Boston: Back Bay Books, 2002.

54 "What Is Net Promoter?," Net Promoter Network (blog),
accessed July 29, 2020,
https://www.netpromoter.com/know/.

55 "Pygmalion (Mythology)." In Wikipedia, July 8, 2020.
https://en.wikipedia.org/w/index.php?title=Pygmalion_(myt
hology)&oldid=966710200.

56 Wasserman, Noam. "The Founder's Dilemma." Harvard
Business Review, February 1, 2008.
https://hbr.org/2008/02/the-founders-dilemma.

57 "Rube goldberg Machine." In Wikipedia, July 18, 2020. https://en.wikipedia.org/w/index.php?title=Rube_goldberg_machine&oldid=968357644.

58 "Occam's Razor." In Wikipedia, July 16, 2020. https://en.wikipedia.org/w/index.php?title=Occam%27s_razor&oldid=968048194.

59 "Definition of INTENDS." Accessed July 22, 2020. https://www.merriam-webster.com/dictionary/intends.

60 "The Best Nike Ads: 13 of the Most Influential of All Time," accessed September 5, 2020, https://www.highsnobiety.com/p/best-nike-ads/.

61 "Amazon.Com: Change or Die: The Three Keys to Change at Work and in Life (9780061373671): Deutschman, Alan: Books." Accessed July 22, 2020. https://www.amazon.com/Change-Die-Three-Keys-Work/dp/0061373672/ref=sr_1_2?dchild=1&keywords=change+or+die&qid=1595470682&sr=8-2.

62 Time. "What Stephen Hawking Said About 'A Brief History of Time.'" Accessed July 22, 2020. https://time.com/5198804/stephen-hawking-obituary-brief-history-of-time/.

63 "Amazon.Com: Change or Die: The Three Keys to Change at Work and in Life (9780061373671): Deutschman, Alan: Books." Accessed July 22, 2020. https://www.amazon.com/Change-Die-Three-Keys-Work/dp/0061373672/ref=sr_1_2?dchild=1&keywords=change+or+die&qid=1595470682&sr=8-2.

64 World Economic Forum. "What Makes Copenhagen the World's Most Bike-Friendly City?" Accessed July 22, 2020. https://www.weforum.org/agenda/2018/10/what-makes-copenhagen-the-worlds-most-bike-friendly-city/.

65 "The E-Cigarette Revolution That Wasn't." Accessed July 22, 2020.
https://www.nationalaffairs.com/publications/detail/the-e-cigarette-revolution-that-wasn%E2%80%99t.

6. The Alchemical Toolkit

66 "107% Rule." In Wikipedia, July 12, 2020.
https://en.wikipedia.org/w/index.php?title=107%25_rule&oldid=967319790.

67 "Amazon.Com 2016 Shareholder Letter." Accessed July 26, 2020.
https://www.sec.gov/Archives/edgar/data/1018724/000119312516530910/d168744dex991.htm.

68 Borison, Rebecca. "Here Are 10 of Amazon's Biggest Failures." TheStreet. Accessed July 26, 2020.
https://www.thestreet.com/investing/stocks/here-are-10-of-amazon-s-biggest-failures-13364106.

69 Heath, Chip, and Dan Heath. Made to Stick: Why Some Ideas Survive and Others Die. 1st edition. New York: Random House, 2007.

70 Heath, Chip, and Dan Heath. Made to Stick: Why Some Ideas Survive and Others Die. 1st edition. New York: Random House, 2007.

7. The Alchemist's Journey

71 "Jennifer Doudna." In Wikipedia, June 25, 2020.
https://en.wikipedia.org/w/index.php?title=Jennifer_Doudna&oldid=964357237.

CPSIA information can be obtained
at www.ICGtesting.com
Printed in the USA
LVHW080356180121
676770LV00007B/142